AF254328

A MANUAL OF WOOD CARVING

By

Charles G. Leland

Revised By

John. J. Holtzapffel

1891

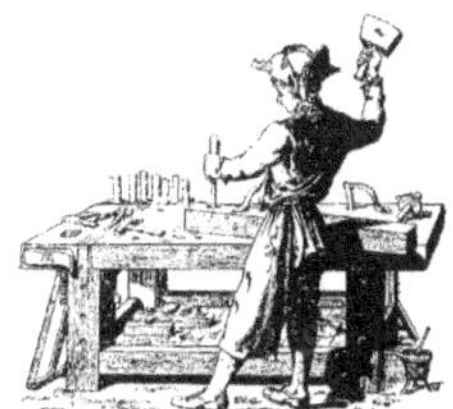

The Toolemera Press
History Preserved

www.toolemera.com

A MANUAL OF WOOD CARVING
by Charles. G. Leland; Revised by John J. Holtzapffel
Charles Scribner's Sons, New York
Original publication date: 1891

International Standard Book Number
ISBN: 978-0-9831500-5-3
Trade Paper

Published by
The Toolemera Press
Massachusetts, U.S.A.

www.toolemera.com

Manufactured in the United States of America

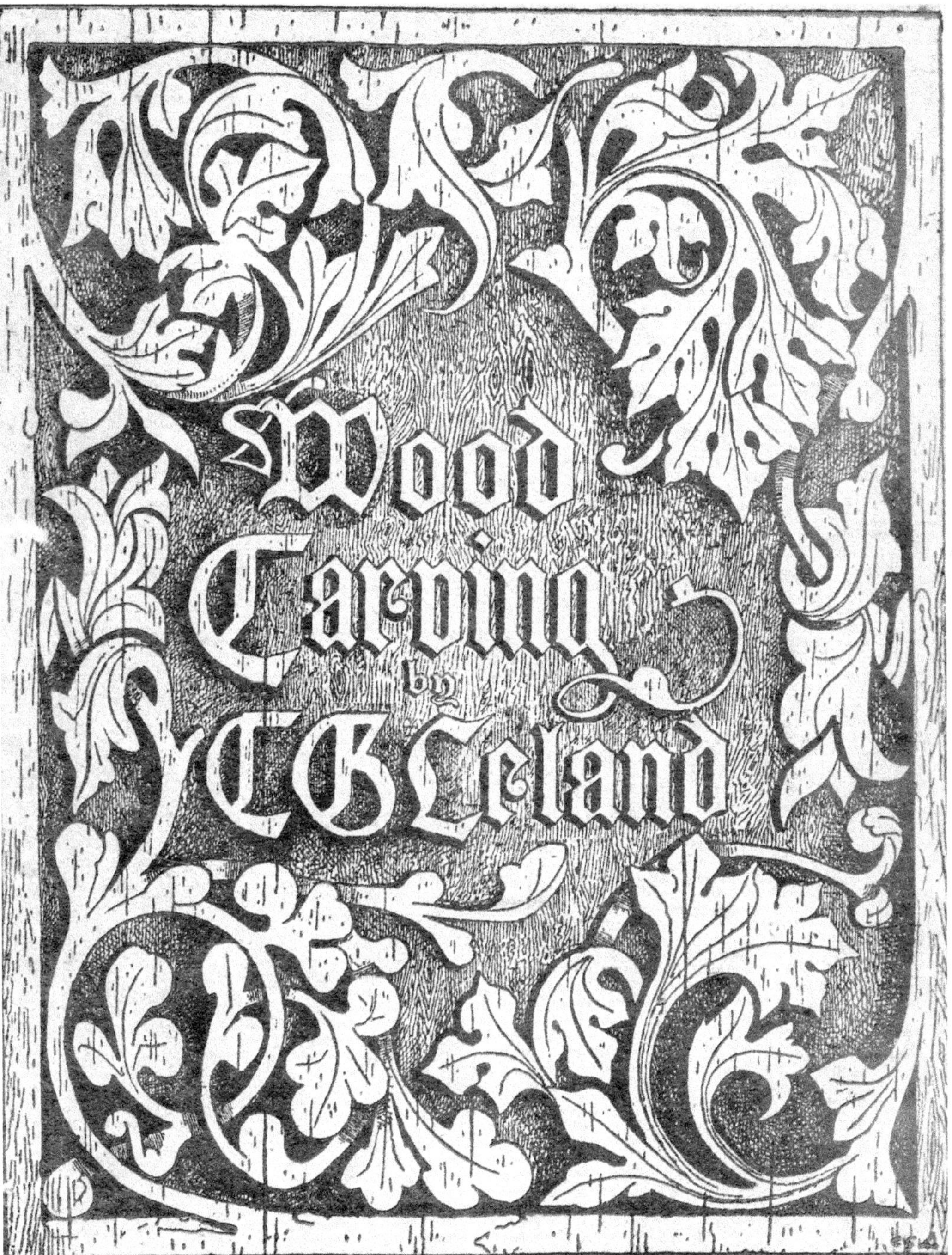
Wood
Carving
by
CG Leland

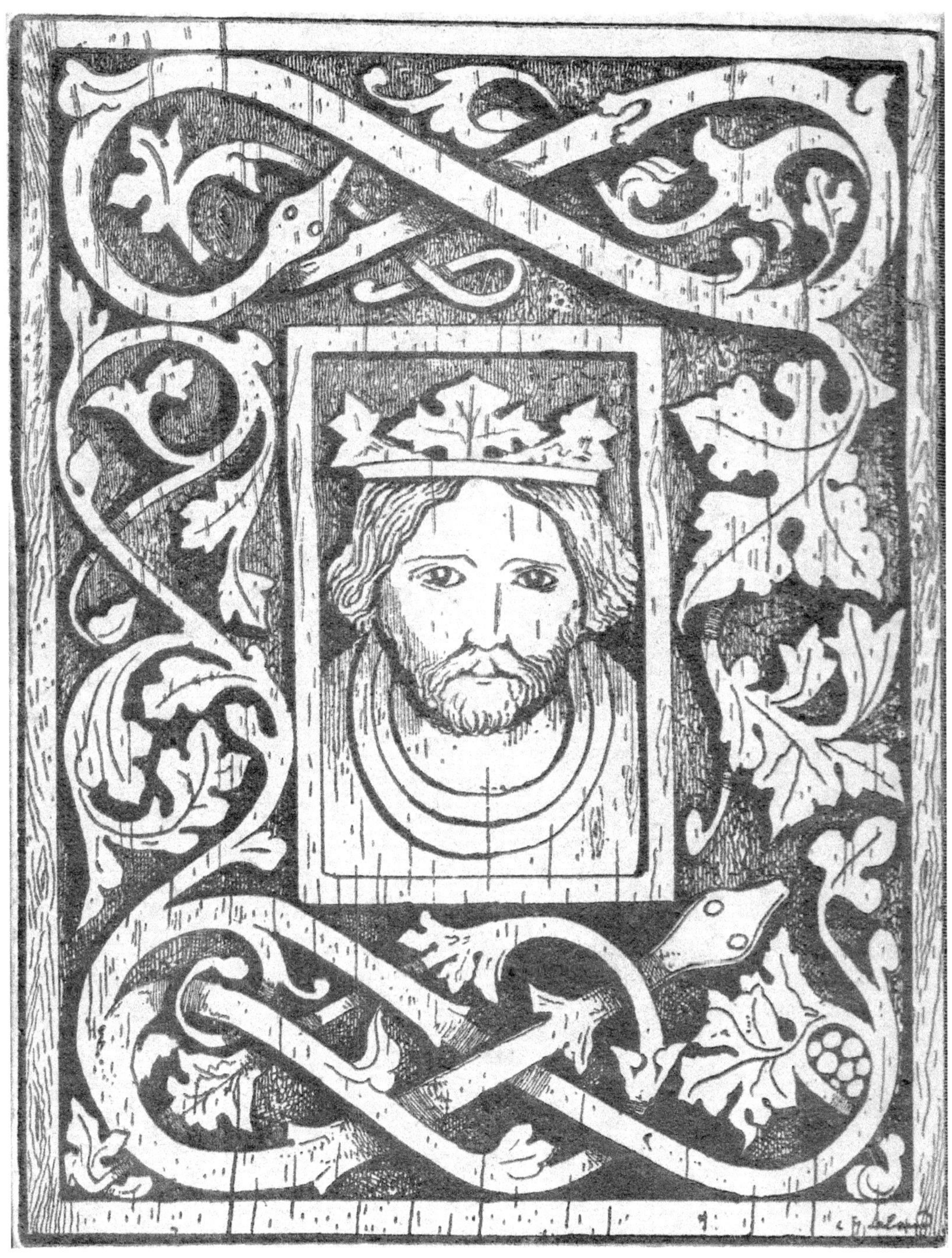

Introduction to the Toolemera edition of *A Manual Of Wood Carving*.

Charles Godfrey Leland was, by his own admission, a distinguished linguist, folklorist, historian, educator and author. He included in his accomplishments a knowledge of witchcraft and sorcery along with a close familiarity with various ethnic cultures who, according to Leland, viewed him as a member rather than as an outsider.

Born 1824 in Philadelphia, Pennsylvania and died 1903, Leland was educated at Princeton and in various institutions in Europe. He pursued the mystical beliefs popular at the time, studied "lesser" cultures as a career and wrote numerous texts based upon his travels and studies. His books and articles were both accepted and criticized during his lifetime and thereafter for their first person content as well as for the extent to which his personal beliefs colored his writings.

Leland later became involved with the Transcendentalist movement and later converted to a Pantheistic view of faith that encompassed an Anglo-Saxon sense of mythology. In other words, he was a scion of the newly wealthy merchant class of the day.

Of his numerous books, seven were focused on the burgeoning Arts & Craft movement of the late 19th century:

- Drawing And Designing
- A Manual Of Wood Carving
- Elementary Metal Work

- The Minor Arts: Porcelain Painting, Wood-Carving, Stenciling, Modeling, Mosaic Work, Etc.

- Leather Work: A Practical Manual For Learners

- A Manual Of Mending And Repairing

- Practical Education

A Manual Of Wood Carving was first published by Charles Scribner's Sons, New York, in 1891, with a revision by John J. Holtzapffel, who added a chapter on the use of the hand saw. it was later published by Whittaker & Co., London. *Wood Carving* was an expansion of Leland's earlier book of 1890: *The Minor Arts: Porcelain Painting, Wood-Carving, Stenciling, Modeling, Mosaic Work, Etc.*

A Manual Of Wood Carving displays Leland's interest in Celtic, Anglo-Saxon and Gothic ornamentation. While the selection of carvings ranges from the heavily Gothic through the Celtic, they always retain the naturalistic themes that typified the Arts & Crafts ideals.

Leland was an artist and carver in his own right, as indicated by a number of his well executed designs in *A Manual Of Wood Carving*. His descriptive text, unlike many self-educational books of the period, is fully developed and progresses in a sensible manner. His intent is to provide the student of wood carving with the technical foundations of the craft as well as to introduce the philosophical themes of craft work.

Of interest is that Whittaker & Co, London, also published the books of David Denning, author of *The Art And Craft Of Cabinet-Making*, another popular craft book of the late 19th century. Denning's book is offered by Toolemera as part of it's series of Classic Reprints.

Holtzapffel & Co., Charing Cross, London, manufacturer's and purveyors of the finest turning equipment of the day, offered *A Manual Of Wood Carving* for sale at their shop. Given that John J. Holtzapffel added the chapter on hand saws, this is not a surprise.

The sole difference between the 1901 edition of *A Manual Of Wood Carving* and the earlier editions is the addition of a single, 19 line page at the very end addressing Pressed And Raised Wood.

Reprints From shop.Toolemera.com

- The Cabinet Maker And Upholsterer's Guide, 1829 by J. Stokes

- Mechanick Exercises, 1703 by Joseph Moxon

- The Mechanic's Companion, 1850 by Peter Nicholson

- The Circle Of The Mechanical Arts, 1813 by Thomas Martin

- Wood Carving, 1896 by Joseph Phillips

- Woodwork Tools And How To Use Them, 1922 by William Fairham

- Woodwork Joints, 1920 by William Fairham

- Cabinet Construction, 1930 by J. C. S. Brough

- Furniture Making: Advanced Projects In Woodwork, 1912 by Ira Griffith

- The Painter, Gilder, And Varnisher's Companion, 1850 Edited by Henry Carey Baird

- Our Workshop, 1866 by Temple Thorold

- Carpentry And Joinery For Amateurs, 1879 by James Lukin

- The Art Of Mitring, 1892 by Owen Maginnis

- Working Drawings Of Colonial Furniture, 1912, F. J. Bryan

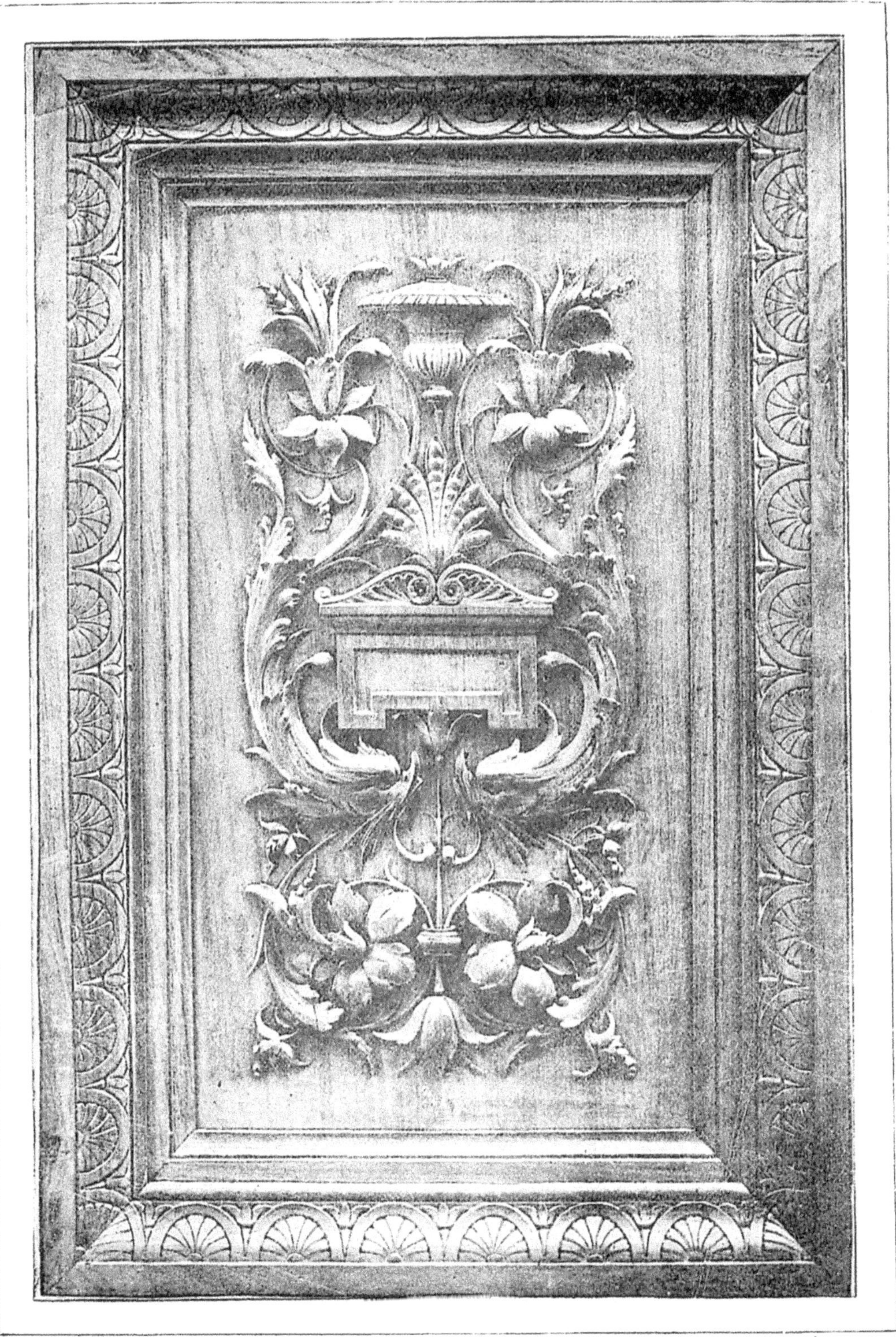

PANEL.

P. 124.

A MANUAL OF WOOD CARVING

BY

CHARLES G. LELAND, F.R.L.S., M.A

*Late Director of the Public Industrial Art School of Philadelphia; Member
(Committee) of the Home Arts and Ind. Assn. ; also Comm. Member of the
French-American and Hungarian Folk Lore Societies ; Pres.
British Gypsy Lore Soc., &c.; Author of " The Minor
Arts," " Twelve Manuals of Arts," " Practical
Education," " Album and Handbook of
Repoussé Work," &c. &c*

REVISED BY

JOHN J. HOLTZAPFFEL

*Associate Member of the Institute of Civil Engineers, London ; Corresponding
Member of the Franklin Institute, Philadelphia; Member of the
British Horological Institute ; Examiner, City and Guilds
of London ; Institute for the Advancement of
Technical Education, &c. &c*

NEW YORK

CHARLES SCRIBNER'S SONS

1891

Press of J. J. Little & Co.
Astor Place, New York

PUBLISHERS' NOTE.

THIS manual, like that on Drawing and Designing, previously
published, is intended to form one of a series in furtherance of
the principles set forth in Mr. Leland's work on "Practical
Education." It has rarely happened that a volume such as this
latter, proposing (as one critic declared) nothing less than a
complete revolution in Education, has been so favourably
received by the public, and so highly approved by competent
authorities, as was the case with it. Should it be unknown to
any friends of educational reform into whose hands this handbook may fall, it is to be hoped that they will think it worth
while to make themselves acquainted with the principles upon
which Mr. Leland's practical manuals are based.

As regards this in particular, it may be observed that it is
almost the only one which treats Wood-carving in a general and
extended sense, and regards it as an art widely applicable to
ornamentation, and not one confined to small *chefs-d'œuvre* and
prize toys, facsimiles of fruit and leaves, or the like. It is the
first book in which the sweep-cut, which is the very soul of all
good and bold carving, has ever been described. It may be
added that the work has derived great advantage from the
friendly interest taken in it by Mr. John J. Holtzapffel, for
which the thanks of both author and publishers are due.

CONTENTS.

LIST OF PLATES.

Wood-Carving.

INTRODUCTION.

WOODS, TOOLS, AND SHARPENING.

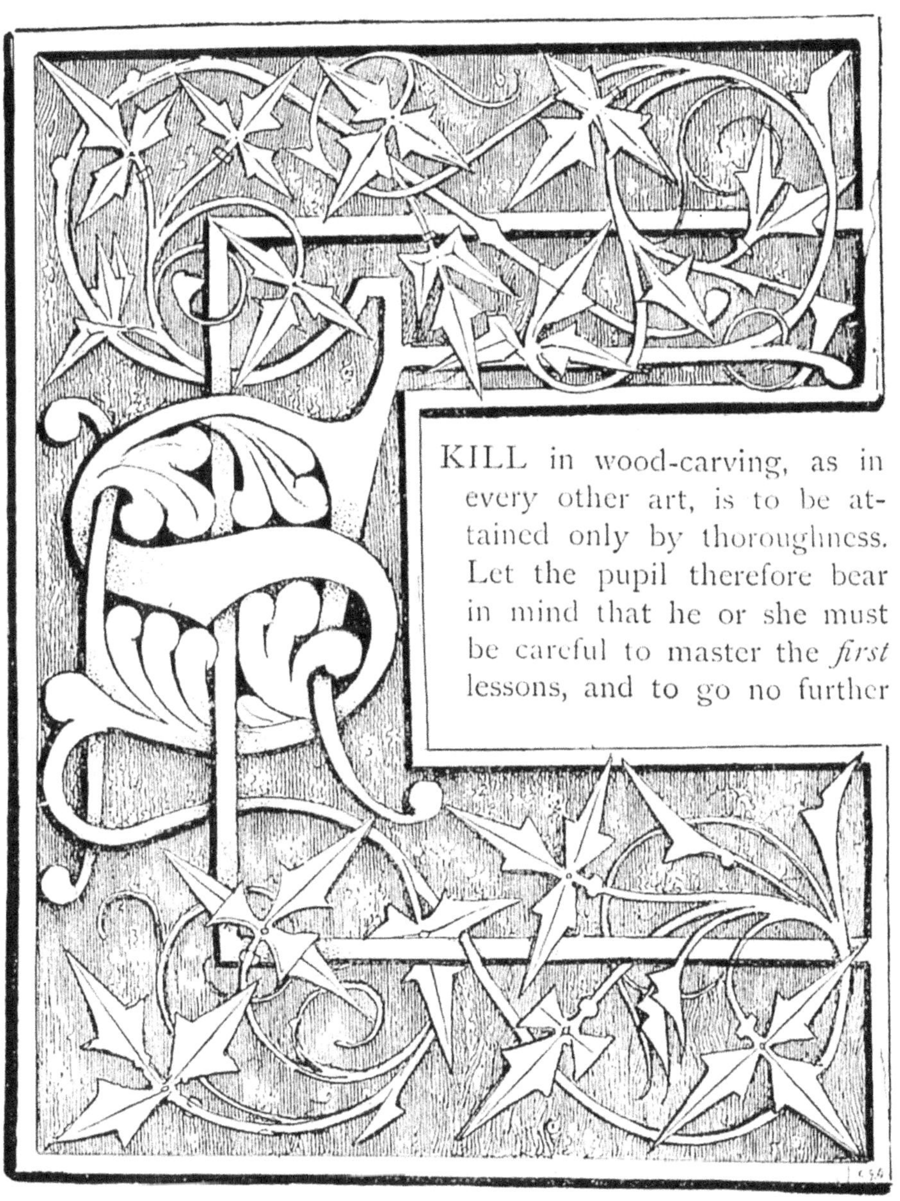

KILL in wood-carving, as in every other art, is to be attained only by thoroughness. Let the pupil therefore bear in mind that he or she must be careful to master the *first* lessons, and to go no further until these can be executed with ease and accuracy. This will be greatly aided if the book is read with care, and not used for mere reference.

TEACHERS will please observe that the work is in a regular series of progressive lessons, the first being extremely easy ; and that these lessons lead so gradually one to another that the last are no harder than the first to one who has gone on carefully from the beginning. This will be found to aid teaching and self-instruction greatly.

Every item of information will be found under its proper head, and not scattered here and there through different chapters : for every lesson is complete in itself, and from the first the pupil is taught how to produce some satisfactory work of its kind. Thus, indenting or stamping, which can be learned at once, and grooving with a gouge, which is not more difficult, are capable of producing very beautiful decoration even if the worker goes no further. No writer has, indeed, ever seriously considered what valuable and varied results may be produced by these simple processes.

Finally, the author has endeavoured in these pages to treat wood-carving not merely as a fine art, whose chief aim is to produce specimens of fancy work for exhibitions, and facsimiles of flowers, never to be touched, but also to qualify the learner for a calling, and what nine-tenths of all practical wood-carving really consists of, that is, house and other large decoration, and of work which is to be perhaps painted, and exposed to the air. There is no reason why the artist should not be prepared to undertake figure-heads for ships, garden gates, cornices for roofs and rooms, dados, door panels, and similar work, as well as mere drawing-room toys, which should have no finish save the delicate touch of the cutting tool.

The author would observe as regards this work that he has been under very great obligation to Mr. John J. HOLTZAPFFEL,

Assoc. M. Inst. C.E., whose name is so well known to all workers in wood and metal, for revisions, suggestions, and addition of the chapter on the use of the saw in carving. He is also indebted to Mr. CADDY, teacher of wood-carving in Brighton for valuable suggestions.

TOOLS AND IMPLEMENTS. The first and most important is a strong, and, if possible, a *heavy* table or bench. If the pupil cannot afford this, an ordinary small kitchen table must be found. It should be used for carving alone, as it will be necessary to bore holes and drive screws into it. But if a table cannot be spared for this, the pupil must make shift by putting a board at least an inch in thickness on a common table, and fastening it with clamps. At a more advanced stage he will carve standing up at a higher bench, or with his work on a stand. Pupils in wood-carving "shops" often carve standing from the beginning.

Carving Tools are generally divided into two classes: chisels, which are flat at the end and in the blade; and gouges, which are hollow. Among professional wood-carvers the former is generally known as a *firmer*, in order to distinguish it from the chisel used by carpenters. A carver's chisel is always ground on *both* sides, so as to form a wedge like a very high, steep roof (*a*), while that of the carpenter is a stouter implement, its edge being like a wedge which is flat on *one* side (*b*), as it is only ground on the other. The object of grinding carvers' chisels on *both* sides is that there are many cuts which cannot be executed by a carpenter's chisel at all, or at least not with ease, for one would be obliged, while using it, to continually turn it around.

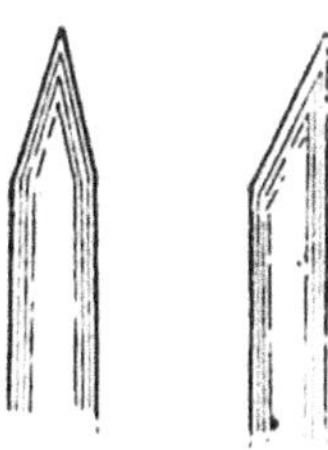

a   *b*

Carver's Chisels or Firmers, Fig. 1 *b*, are of many and all sizes, from an inch in breadth down to the "pick," which, across the end or edge, is no wider than a small hyphen (-). To these may be added the "skew-chisels," also called "skews" or

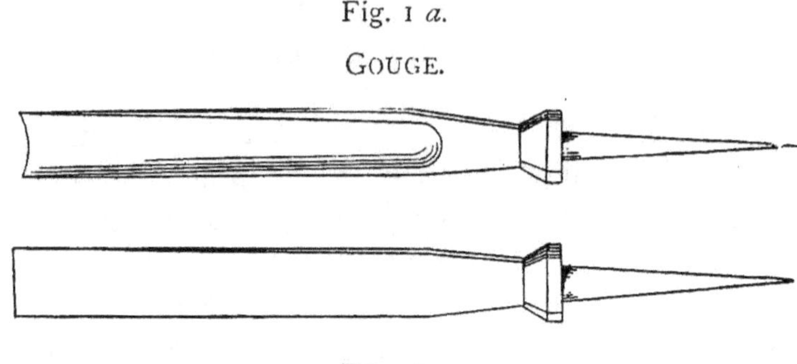

Fig. 1 *a.*

GOUGE.

FIRMER.

"corner-firmers," which are firmers ground off diagonally, so that the point is on one side. These are also sharpened on both sides.

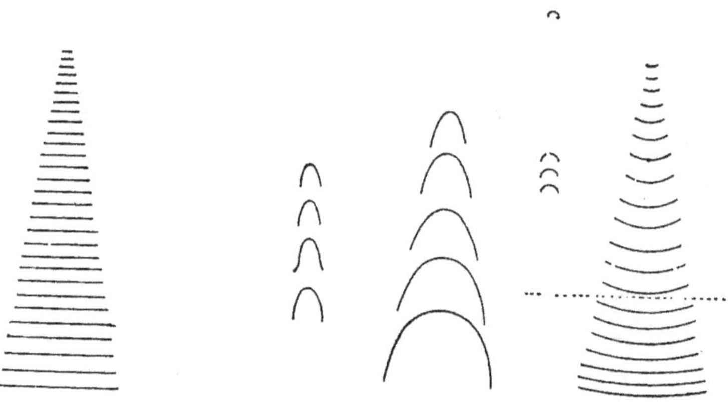

Fig. 1 *b.*   FIRMERS.   Figs. 2-5.   GOUGES.

Gouges, Figs. 2-5, are chisels more or less rounded. These, of all widths, vary from the *extra flat*, which is so slightly curved that it might at a casual glance be taken for an ordinary chisel, to the ordinary "flat." A little more bend or convexity gives the *scroll gouge*. A semi-circle or any narrower portion of the same curve is a *hollow gouge*, the smaller sizes of which are called *veiners*, the very smallest of the latter being known as *eye-tools*. There are some differences of names for these among writers, as well as workmen, but for all practical purposes the terms here used may be accepted, and are understood by all who sell the tools.

Bent Tools. Both chisels and gouges are made straight, or bent or curved in the shank. It often happens that in deep

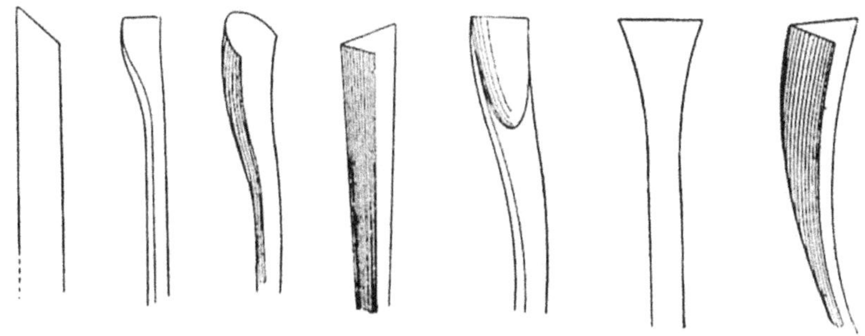

Fig. 6. BENT TOOLS.

cutting, or in hollowed spaces, it is impossible to cut with an implement having a straight shaft, while with one differently shaped the wood can be easily removed, Fig. 6.

Holdfasts.—Carver's Screws, and *Clamps, Hand Screws, Bench Screws, &c.* As the carver holds his tool with one hand and directs it with the other, it is evident that some means must be taken to secure in place the piece of work which he cuts. I. The simplest method of doing this is to drive three or four nails or screws into the table at a convenient distance. The work may be held between these to prevent its slipping.

II. HOLDFASTS.—*Clamps* or *Cramps*, Fig. 7. These cramps

are small iron frames, like three sides of a square, with a
screw in the under limb. They are used on the edge of the
table to hold the work firmly down to its surface; two or more
are always employed. Their fault is that they indent and
damage the work; a piece of waste wood may be interposed
between the work and the upper limb to prevent this, but such
a guard is generally in the way and otherwise objectionable.
Hand Screws, Figs. 8 and 9, are a far better tool, entirely free
from the above-named objection. They consist of two strips of

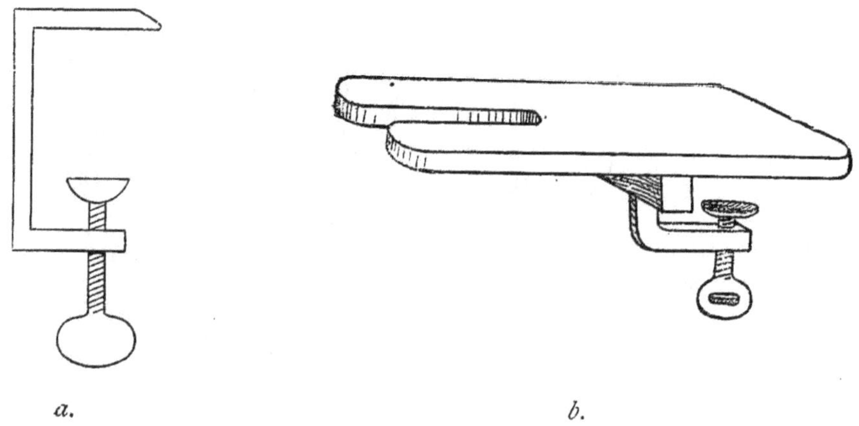

a.   *b.*

Fig. 7. HOLDFAST AND SAW TABLE.

hard wood rounded at the one end, or jaws, and two screws, also
of wood, one of which passes through both jaws, and the other
through only one; the end of this second screw entering a recess
made in the other jaw to retain it in position. To use them the
handles are grasped firmly in the two hands, and the hands are
revolved around one another away from you, which causes the
jaws to open exactly parallel with one another. When the
opening between the jaws equals the thickness of the work and
the table, the hand screws are slipped over them, and the second

screw then alone receives an extra half turn, this throws the jaws slightly out of parallelism, and effects a powerful grip upon the work at their points. They are exceedingly powerful also in

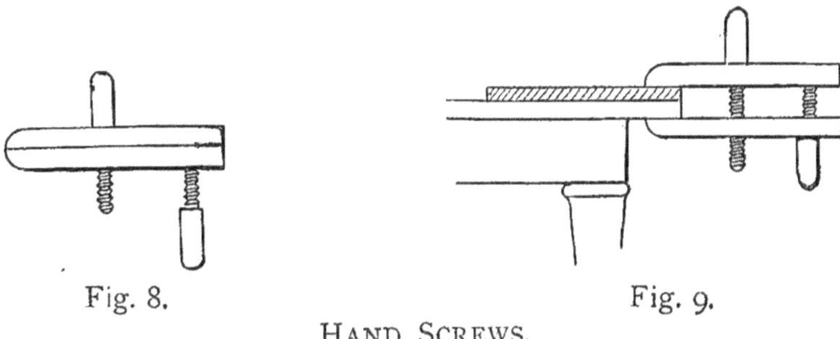

Fig. 8. Fig. 9.

HAND SCREWS.

holding work for gluing together and other purposes, and are made of all sizes.

III. *Carvers' Screws*, Fig. 10. These are iron screws about 12 or 14 in. long, with a finer pointed screw, like that of a gimlet, at the one end, and a square at the other; on the screw is a winged or fly nut. To use them the point is screwed firmly into the under side of the work, with the fly nut removed and used as a lever by one of the holes in its wings placed on the square on the end of the shaft. The shaft is then passed through a hole made through the top of the bench or table, and the fly nut replaced on the screw below the table to fix the work down to it The screws are long, which is sometimes convenient, but if the work be thin it is usual to put a block of waste wood on the shaft before the fly nut, to avoid the tedium of having to screw the latter up a long way. Slackening the nut enables the work to be turned round to any required position, and there is nothing above the table except the work.

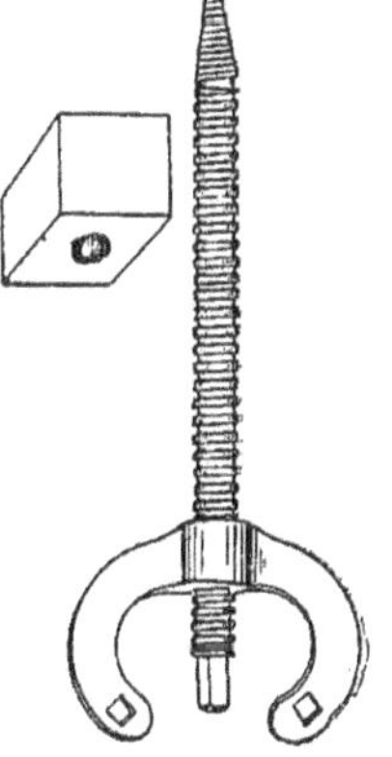

Fig. 10.

CARVERS' SCREWS.

IV. *Snibs or Dogs*, Figs. 11, 12. These are pieces of wood screwed down to the table, which hold the panel or other piece of work by a projection. They are easily made by simply saw-

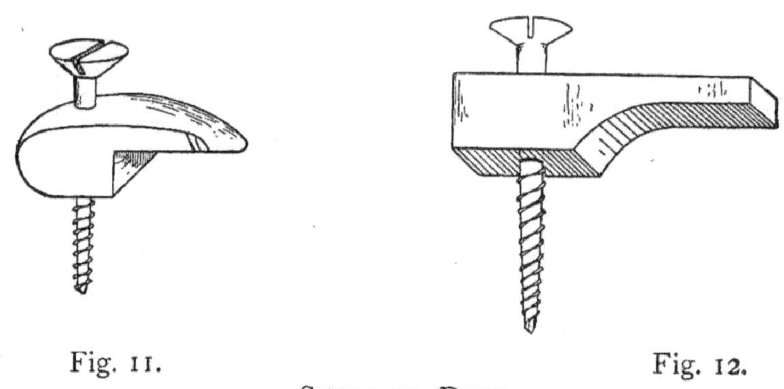

Fig. 11.   Fig. 12.

Snibs or Dogs.

ing out a piece of wood fairly corresponding in thickness to the panel.

V. Take an ordinary " button," Fig. 13, such as is common on cupboards in country cottages to fasten the door. Saw out a piece of the panel, one or more inches square. Put the screw through the button and turn it over the panel and the little waste piece of wood. Two or more of these will hold the work perfectly fast.

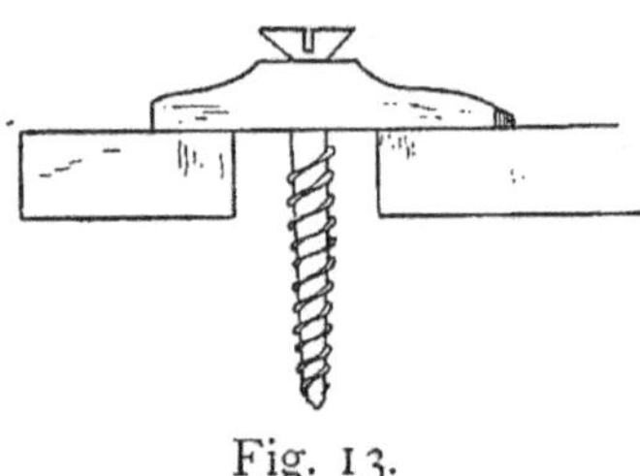

Fig. 13.

VI. The simplest method of all is to leave about an inch at either end of the panel and pass screws through these extra portions into the table. When the work is carved these ends may be sawn off.

The Scratch, Fig. 14. This is a very convenient and ingenious tool. " It is used," says J. S. Gibson (" The Wood-Carver,"

Edinburgh, 1889), "for running small mouldings and hollows. Where the lines are long and straight it makes finer work than is possible by means of gouges. The cutters are made from pieces of steel barely 1-16th of an inch thick. Broken pieces of saws are generally used for cutters. They must be tightly fixed in the stock. It is worked backwards and forwards gently. When the cutters are filed to the required shape, they have to be finished with a slip stone to take out the file marks. They are sharpened straight across the edges."

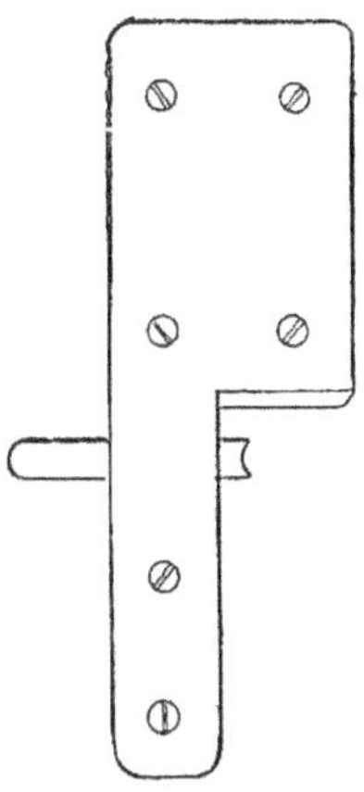

Fig. 14. SCRATCH.

The Router, Fig. 15. This is a small copy of the joiner's plane of the same name. It consists of a block of wood with a perfectly flat sole; a hole through it at an angle carries the cutter and the wedge by which it is fixed. It is employed for flattening the groundwork after that has been partially excavated with the chisels. The sole of the router rests upon any margins left of the original surface, and being worked about over the ground, the fixed projection of the cutter rapidly reduces the latter to one true level. These routers are made from about nine inches long in the sole to about three inches, the smallest, which little tools have cutters about 1-8th of an inch wide.

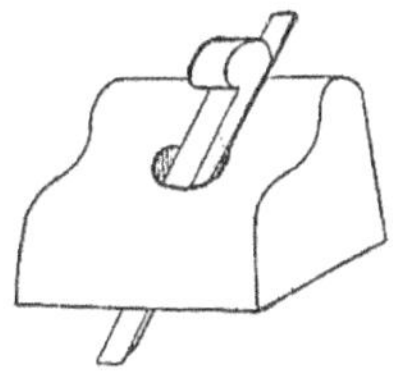

Fig. 15. ROUTER.

Saws. These are of various kinds; perhaps the most useful is the Fret Bow Saw, Fig. 16. This consists of a light thin steel frame with screw jaws, at the open end in which the thin saw-blades are clamped. The handle is also formed as a screw, by which its jaw can be advanced about an inch towards its fellow. To place the saw in position for work, the end of the handle is screwed round until its jaw has advanced about an inch, the saw is then fixed in the opposite jaw by its thumb-screw, then in the handle jaw in the same way, after which the handle is turned until its jaw has travelled back again the distance it had previously advanced, thus straining the saw by the tension of the steel spring saw-frame.   This saw is very useful for removing superfluous pieces from the outline, both in flat works and when carving in the round, as will be explained ; its primary purpose is for cutting out pierced and buhl and fretwork, but for such work, as the apertures cut do not lways cut out to the edges, a drill is required to pierce holes to thread the saw through the work before it is placed in the second jaw to strain it.   Fig. 16

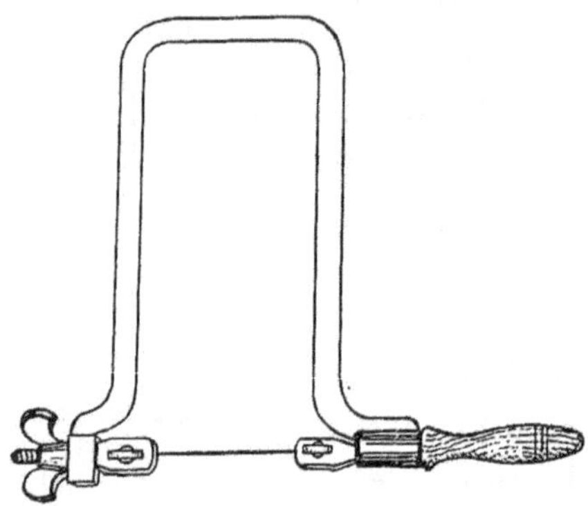

Fig. 16.   FRET BOW SAW.

is required for pierced work laid down on a ground and then carved, a style of carving which will be described.   The ordinary joiners " dovetail " or " tenon " saws, their blades with stiff backs, are required, and are almost indispensable for cutting off portions of the work and trimming it to shape ; these saws are too well known to require description.

In addition to the tools already described, the pupil will need for more and varied work the following :—I. *The Spade Chisel,* and *Spade Gouge.*   These are very light, and are used for finishing by hand, as, for instance, in cutting around grapes or plums or in fine work.   II. *Knuckle-bends,* Fig. 17.   These are gouges scooped or bent in a curve like a knuckle.   III. *The Macaroni Tool,* Fig. 18.   This is like the three sides of a square.   It is for removing wood on each side of a vein or leaf, or similar delicate work.   It is not very commonly used.   IV. *The Parting*

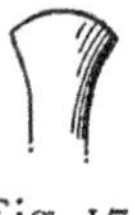

Fig. 17.
KNUCKLE-
BEND.

Tool or V, *straight or curved.* This is a useful tool for out-lining a pattern or veining leaves. Beginners find it, like the Macaroni, rather difficult to sharpen, or to keep an edge on it. It must not be used recklessly for carving, as it is apt to break unless handled with care. It should be kept with a cork on the end.

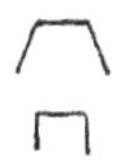

Fig. 18.
MACARONI
TOOLS.

It is a question among experts as to whether the tools for beginners should have long or short handles, which is as sensible as if they should debate whether the pupils should have large or small hands. General Seaton, who is in other matters a good authority, declares that "small, short, neatly-turned box-wood handles must be avoided ; they are nearly useless. Get good-sized beech or ash handles quite five inches long, and if the steel is four or four and a half inches long you will have a really serviceable tool." Common sense teaches that between a child or a young lady who has a palm "the size of a cardinal's seal" (to borrow a simile from Benvenuto Cellini), and a work-man who would burst a number ten glove, there must be very great differences in the size of handles, and it is certain that for young beginners short ones are to be advised. If they are not to be obtained ready made, then take an ordinary long handle, saw it off to the requisite length, say from three to three and a half inches, round the sharp edge of the wood, firstly with a knife or chisel, then with a rasp, and finish it off with glass-paper. See that the tools when set into the handles are *well ringed* and *firm*. In most shops it is usual to sharpen them if it be required. After becoming accustomed to such handles the pupil may, as he progresses, familiarize himself with those which are in general use.

There is really only one *trouble* in wood-carving. This is the sharpening the tools, and keeping them in good condition. For this the grindstone and oilstone are indispensable, and the beginner must take pains to learn to sharpen his tools well and readily.

SHARPENING. Tools which are as yet unground, or which have had the edge broken, may, with patience and care, be sharpened on a harsh flat stone, but round grindstones which revolve with a handle are not dear; you can, however, always get your tools ground by any carpenter. Every carver should therefore, if possible, own one of these grindstones. It will serve as well for a large class as for an individual. The next indispensable is the *oilstone*. This is to be found of different kinds; the ordinary Turkey stone, set in a block of wood, will answer for firmers, skews, and flat gouges, for finer tools the best Arkansas stones may be employed. Before using one, let fall on it a few drops of oil, which is to be kept in a small can with a narrow spout, made expressly for such dropping. Have a coarse rag, and when you have done with the stone, always wipe it clean of the oil. Take great care not to wear a hollow in the middle of the stone. It is by far the best plan to get some wood-carver or carpenter to show you how to sharpen the tools. There are very few places where there is not somebody who can teach this art. It is usual to have a box-cover to the oilstone, which should always be over it when not in use, to prevent dust from settling on the surface. A very little dust indeed combined with the oil is a great hindrance to sharpening.

Slips. These are pieces of Arkansas, Turkey, and other stones, made of a variety of shapes, to fit the inside of such tools as cannot be sharpened on a flat surface, like that of oil-stone. They require great care in handling lest the fingers be cut. To avoid this, take a piece of wood, and cut a deep groove in it, exactly adapted to hold the stone firmly, leaving as much of it projecting as may be required for use, Fig. 19. If you cannot obtain a slip exactly suited to

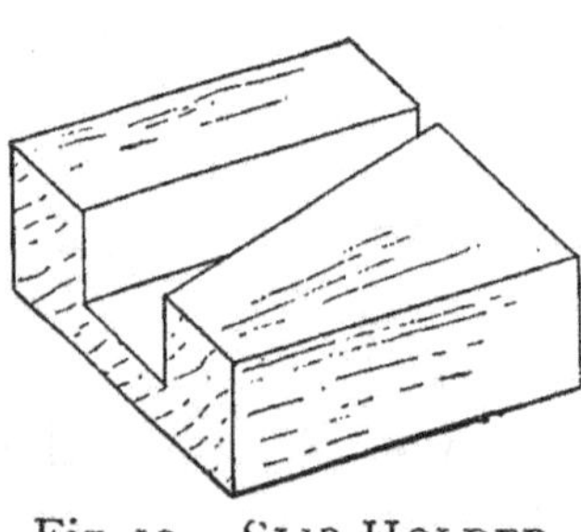

Fig. 19.   SLIP HOLDER.

any particular tool, then grind or cut it to shape on the grind-stone or with a file; some carvers use a very coarse whetstone adapted to this purpose. The safe method of using a slip when not mounted in wood is to " lay the back of the gouge at an inch and a half from the edge on the edge of the table; the edge of the tool must be slightly raised, and the slip can then be applied with perfect safety and with great effect." (Seaton.) The V, or parting tool, is difficult to sharpen because, until one has had practice with it, it is hard to cut down each side in *exact* uniformity with the other. For this it is necessary to have a slip ground to a V edge, so as to exactly fit the inside of the tool.

The Strap. This is a piece of hard, smooth leather, glued on a flat bit of board. This may be prepared with sweet oil and emery powder, or Tripoli, to be renewed as occasion requires, or with a preparation of lard and crocus powder. Emery paste sold at the tool-shop will answer for all ordinary work. When no strap is at hand a final sharp, or a razor edge, may be given even on a smooth pine board, especially if a very little fine air-dust be on it.

Sharpening the tools is like threading the needle in sewing, or putting a point on lead pencils when drawing, something which is a great trouble, and a constant interruption to earnest work, yet which must be constantly seen to. Never go on carving for a second if you find that a tool is growing in the least dull or " scratchy." There can be no good work whatever without really good tools in perfect order.

It may be observed that tools are never ground quite so much *inside* as they are externally. Also that this double grinding gives a sharper cutting-edge; but gouges require very little edging *inside*.

Should the carver be unable to obtain a Turkey or Arkansas stone, he may use smooth slate, or almost any stone which is tolerably hard.

Wood. All wood for carving should be of the best quality, well seasoned, and free as possible from cracks, knots, or other irregularities. Fine white pine or deal, being very easy to cut, is suitable for a beginner. Lime and pear-tree wood, like pine, are even in the grain. American walnut is also easy to cut. It is of a beautiful dark colour, which is much improved by oiling and age. With this, but tougher than the preceding, are beech, elm, and oak. Poplar, yellow deal, and the so-called American wood (known as poplar in America, Middle States) are useful for many kinds of work. The carver should accustom himself, as soon as possible, to oak, as a hard wood is by no means hard to carve as soon as a little skil is acquired. Bone, ivory, and pearl-shell, which at the first effort seems to be almost impenetrable, after a few days are " worked " with great ease.

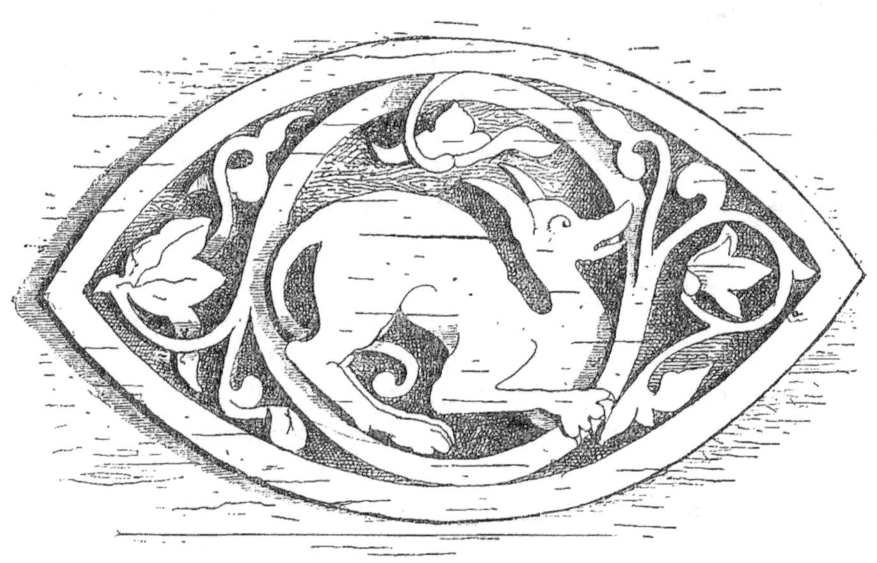

FIRST LESSON.

INDENTING AND STAMPING.

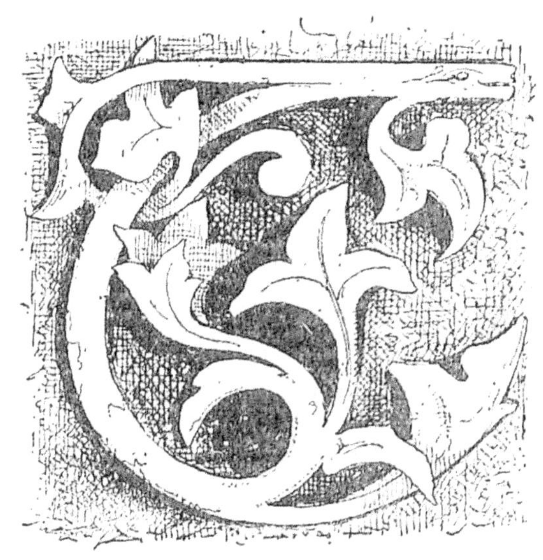

HE first stage in wood-carving is to decorate a flat surface in very low relief by a process which, strictly speaking, is not carving at all. Let the beginner take a panel or thin flat board, let us say one of six inches in breadth, twelve in length, and half an inch or less in thickness. For this kind of work a finely grained, even, and light-coloured wood, such as holly or beech, is preferable. Draw the pattern on paper, of the size intended with a very black and soft lead or crayon pencil, place it with the face to the wood, and turning the edges over, gum them down to the edge of the panel. Then with some very smooth hard object, such as an agate or steel burnisher, an ivory paper-knife, or the end of a rounded and glossy penknife handle, carefully rub the back of the pattern. When this is done remove the paper, and the pattern will be found transferred to the wood. It imperfect, touch it up.

The pupil may now, with a pattern-wheel or tracer, indent or mark a line or narrow groove in the outline of the pattern. The tracer is the same implement of the same name which is used in *repoussé* or brass-sheet or metal-work. Its end is exactly like that of a screw-driver. To manage it properly hold it upright, and run it along, tapping it as it goes with a hammer of iron or wood, Fig. 20. In some countries a stick of wood about six inches in length, and an inch broad at the butt, is used. Where the wheel cannot be employed, as in small corners, use the tracer. The pointed tracer, Fig. 21, used in leather-work, and in carpentry, is often indispensable for the smaller pattern-work.

When the outline is all marked out in a groove, take one of the *stamps*, or grounding punches, shown on Fig. 23, and with the hammer indent the whole background, Fig. 24. If there be corners too small to admit the stamp or stamps for the same pattern, then finish them up with a pointed nail or any point, such as a bodkin. The result will be like the simple design in Fig. 23. When this is done, coat the whole with oil, rub it in, and wipe it off with care. Then with a piece of very soft wood polish only the pattern, and finally rub it off by hand or with a stiff brush. This kind of ornamentation is adapted to the covers of books or albums, as it can be applied to the thinnest sheets of wood.

Fig. 20.

Fig. 21.   POINTED AND EDGED TRACER.

Another way to improve this work is to take the tracer, and smooth down and depress the ground, especially near the pattern edge. This gives an improved relief. Then the ground may be stamped or "matted," Fig. 24. It may be borne in mind that the pupil who masters this process of indenting with wheel, tracers, and stamps, will be quite able to work patterns in damp sheet-leather, since the latter is effected in the same way with the same tools. Nor does the first step in *repoussé* or sheet-brass work differ greatly from it. All the minor arts have a great deal in common ; many of the tools used in one being applicable to others. The pupil who begins with some knowledge of drawing will soon find it easy to work in any material.

The pupil having done this, has an idea of how a pattern is *placed* or *spaced* and contrasted with the ground. He may now take another panel, and having drawn the pattern, cut out the outline in a light groove with a very small gouge or a V tool, or a *firmer*. Let him be very careful to hold the handle in his right hand, and guide the blade with the fingers of the left, *and never to let the latter get before the point.* Do not cut deeply or too rapidly. Before beginning on the pattern, practise cutting grooves on waste wood. Unless this is done the panel will almost certainly be spoiled. It is usual among carvers to begin with cutting the groove with a V tool, but it is well to prepare for this by using the tracer or wheel.

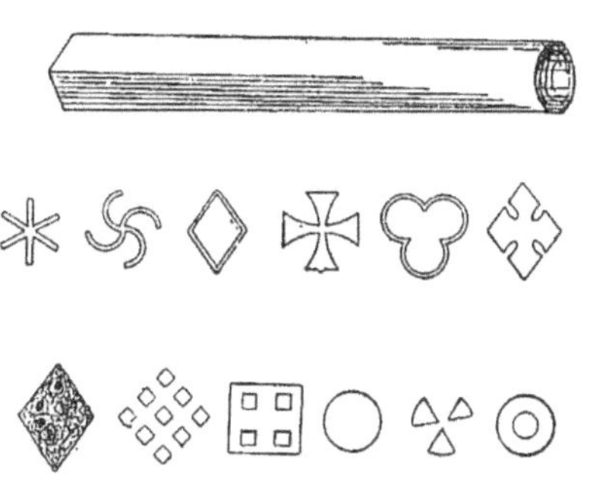

Fig. 23. STAMPS.

Fig. 27 represents the effect of a ground which is indented, and to a degree ornamented, by using round stamps of different patterns and sizes. Very good effects may be produced in this way, which resembles diaper-work.

To clearly recapitulate the process, let me observe: That to begin, the pupil must have a smooth panel without knots or imperfections. The pattern is drawn on this or transferred to it. This pattern should be entirely in outline, without any inside lines or drawing between the outside edges, Fig. 24. Take a wheel or tracer and indent the whole pattern very

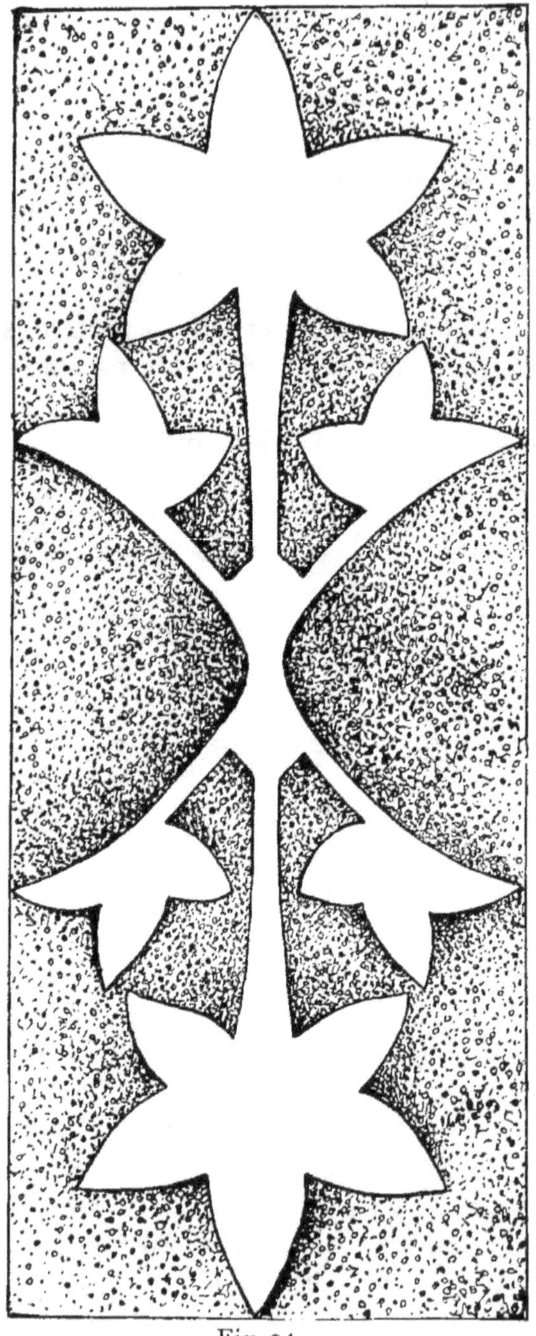

Fig. 24.

carefully and rather deeply, not all at one pressure, but by going twice or thrice over the line. Then with a stamp and hammer indent all the background and the spaces between the edges of the pattern. Having done this once, take another panel and pattern, and instead of *pressing in* the outline with a wheel or tracer, cut it with a parting tool or gouge—not too deeply. Then indent as before, Fig. 25.

This stamping the grounds is often miscalled *diaper* carving, but the diaper is, correctly speaking, a small pattern multiplied to make a ground, and not roughly corrugating or dotting with a bodkin, or pricking. This latter is, of course, indenting. Diapers may be either stamped or carved like any other patterns.

This process of flattening, wheeling, tracing, and stamping wood, though little practised now, was so common in the Middle Ages, that there are very few galleries containing pictures with gold backgrounds in which there are not specimens of it. Very great masters in painting frequently practised it. After gilding the

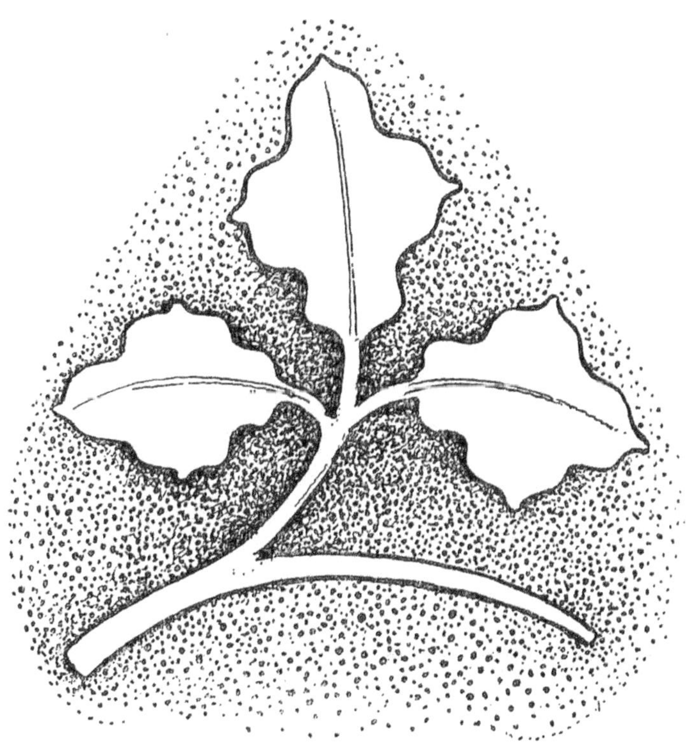

Fig. 25.

ground, they outlined the pattern with a prick-wheel, which is quite like the rowel of a spur, and often traced dotted patterns with the wheel itself on the flat gold. Black or dark brown paint was then rubbed into the dots. Sometimes the stamp was also used, and its marks or holes filled in the same manner. It is not necessary to gild the background to produce a fine effect. First apply a coat of varnish, polish it when dry with finest glass-paper, then apply a coat or two of white oil paint, toned with Naples yellow, and when it is dry work it with wheel-tracers and stamps. When dry polish it again, and rub dark brown paint into all the lines and dots. Cover it with two coats of fine retouching varnish, and the effect will be that of old stamped ivory.

This first lesson may be omitted by those who wish to proceed at once to carving. It is given here because it sets forth the easiest and least expensive manner of ornamenting wood, and one which forms a curious and beautiful art by itself. With it one can acquire a familiarity with the method of transferring patterns to wood, and with the management of the tracer and stamp. The pattern-wheel should be held in the right hand, and guided by the fore-

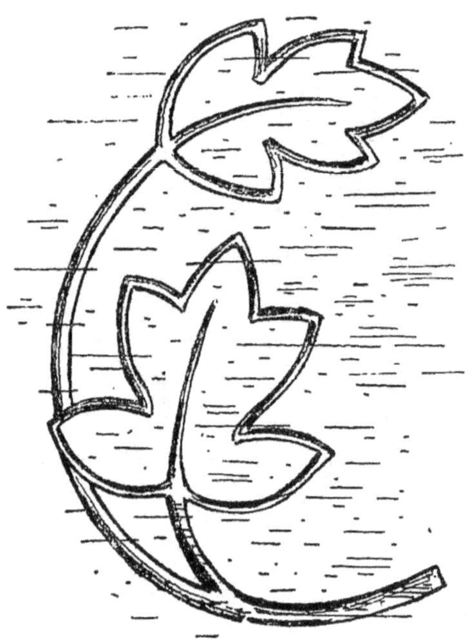

Fig. 26. GOUGE LINES.

finger of the left, which is a good preparatory practice for the chisel and gouge.

While the tools requisite for this work are few and inexpensive, it may be observed that tolerable substitutes may be obtained for them anywhere. Almost any knife-blade, eraser, or screw-driver can be ground into a dull edge which may serve to trace and press the wood, while a spike or very large nail can, with a file, be so crossed at the end as to make a stamp.

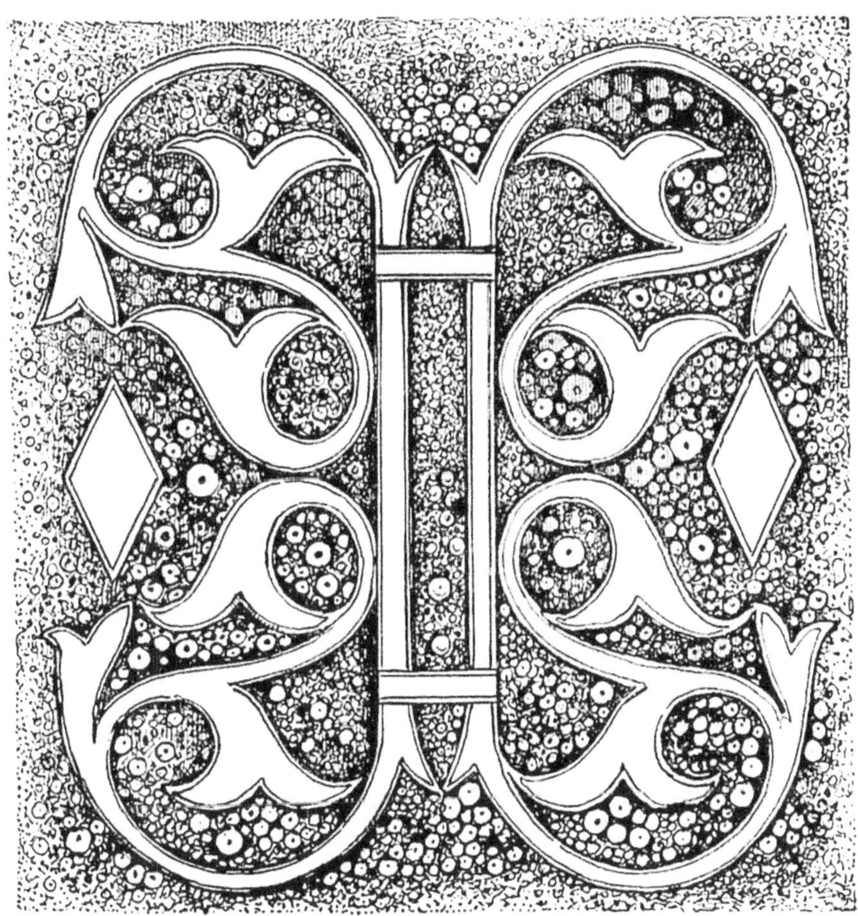

Fig. 27.   INDENTED GROUND.

SECOND LESSON.

CUTTING GROOVES WITH A GOUGE.

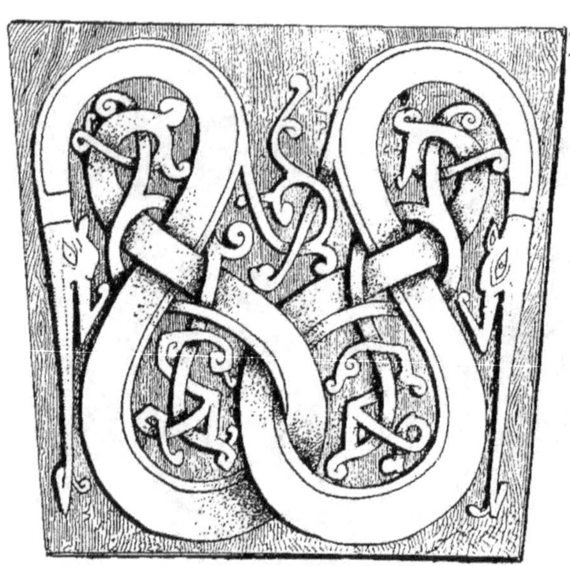

E will now suppose that the pupil has a piece of smooth pine wood, at least six inches by six in size, and half an inch in thickness, fastened to the table before him. Let him draw on it two lines with a lead pencil, across the grain, one-fourth of an inch distant from each other. Then taking a *fluter* or gouge of semi-circular curve, also one-fourth of an inch in diameter, let him carefully cut away the wood between the lines so as to form a semi-circular groove, Fig. 28 *a*. This is not to be effected by cutting all the wood away at once. A very little should be removed at first, so as to make a shallow groove, then this may be cut over again till the incision is perfect. Hold the handle of the tool firmly in the right hand, with the wrist and part of the forearm resting on the bench ; place the two first fingers of the left hand on the face of the blade about an inch from the cutting edge, to direct and act as a stop to prevent the tool advancing too fast. Some place the thumb below the blade, so that it is held between the thumb and the two first fingers.

"Keep your mind on your work—a careless movement may cause a slip of the tool and ruin it." Let every stroke of chisel

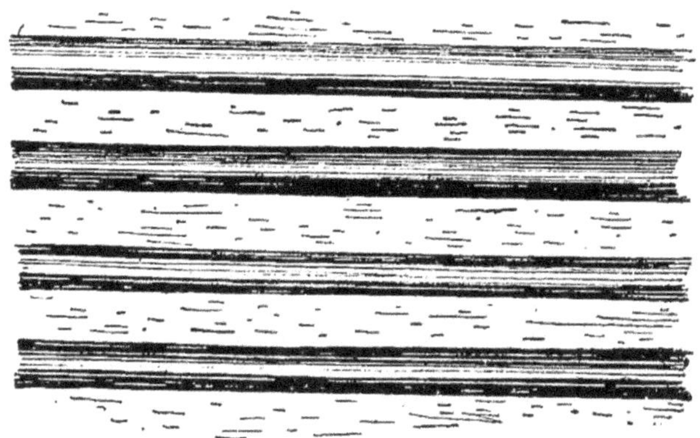

Fig. 28 *a.* STRAIGHT GROOVES.

or gouge be made and regulated by purpose and design, not haphazard, or at random. Think *exactly* what you wish to cut or mean to do, and leave nothing to involuntary action. The habit of doing this may be acquired in the first few lessons, if you try, and when it is acquired all the real difficulty of carving is mastered.

Never attempt to carve anything unless it is fastened to the table. Pupils who do this fall into the habit of holding the panel down with the left hand, and the result is that

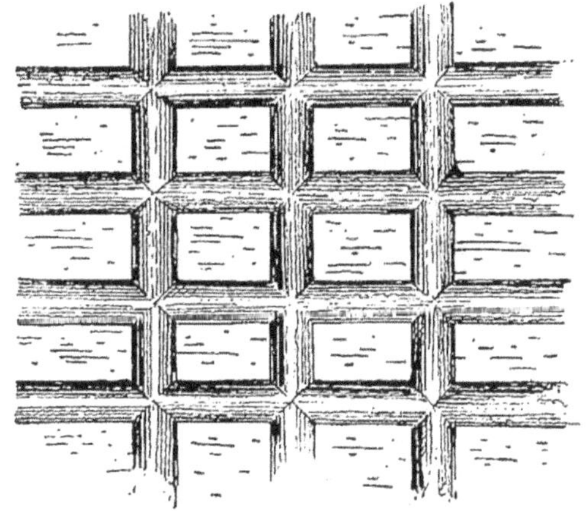

Fig. 28 *b.* CROSS GROOVES.

the tool slips sooner or later, and inflicts a wound which may be serious. Always keep both hands on the tool.

When the pupil shall have cut perhaps twenty straight grooves with great care with the gouge, he may then cut cross-barred grooves, Fig 28 *b*, and then curved ones as in Fig. 29 *a, b, c.*

Two sections of a circle thus intersecting form, as may be seen, a leaf. One, two, or even three lessons may be devoted to this, *but let the pupil go no further until he can cut these grooves*

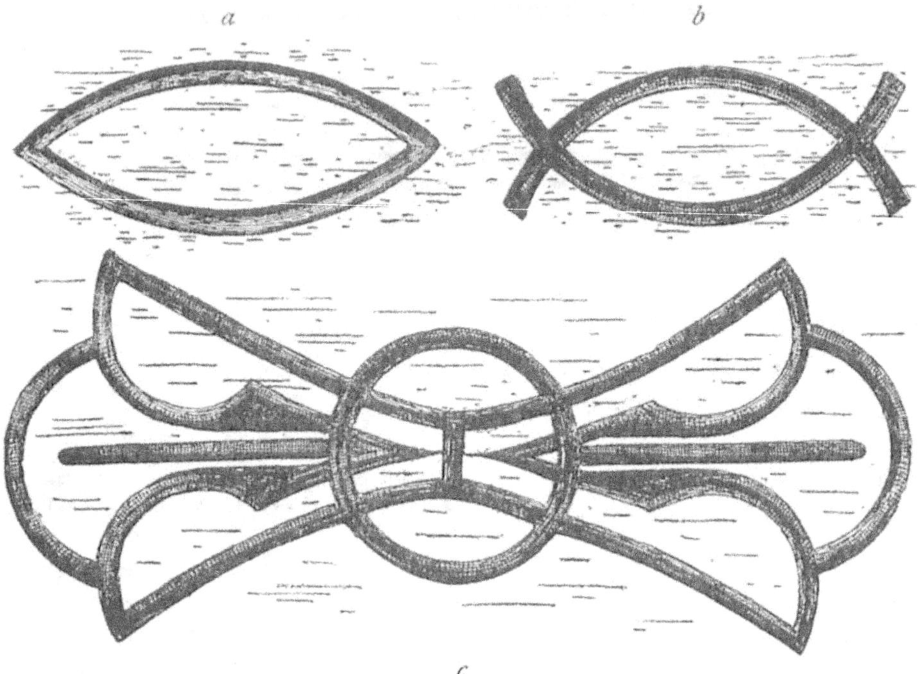

Fig. 29.　Curved and Crossing Grooves.

perfectly. He will then find it excellent practice at odd intervals to carve grooves in circles, spirals, or other forms. Groove-carving may be regarded as line-drawing, for any pattern which can be drawn in simple lines can be of course imitated with a gouge.

Very pretty decorative work may be effected by this gouge-

or furniture, by means of carving, is because all carvers are devoted almost exclusively to more ambitious work, and ignore what may be done with a few tools by the simplest methods.

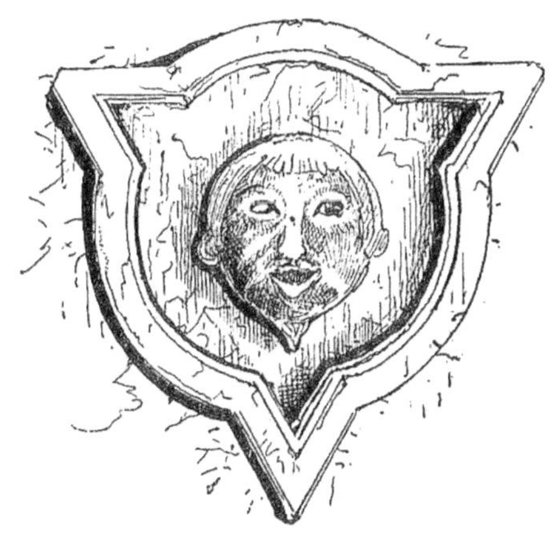

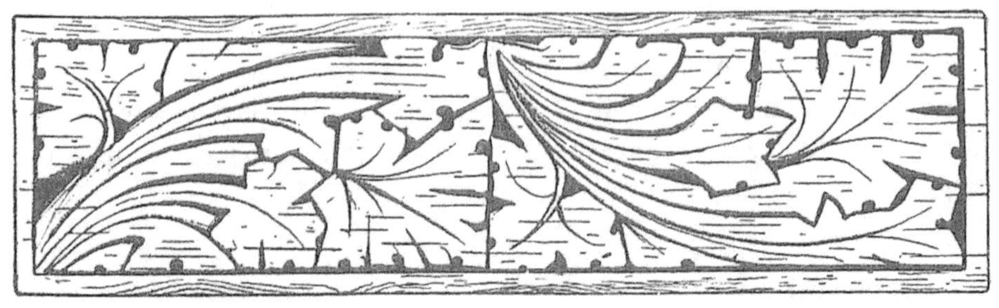

THIRD LESSON.

FLAT PATTERNS MADE WITH CUTS AND LINES—CAVO
RELIEVO OR INTAGLIO RILEVATO (CAVO-CUTTING).

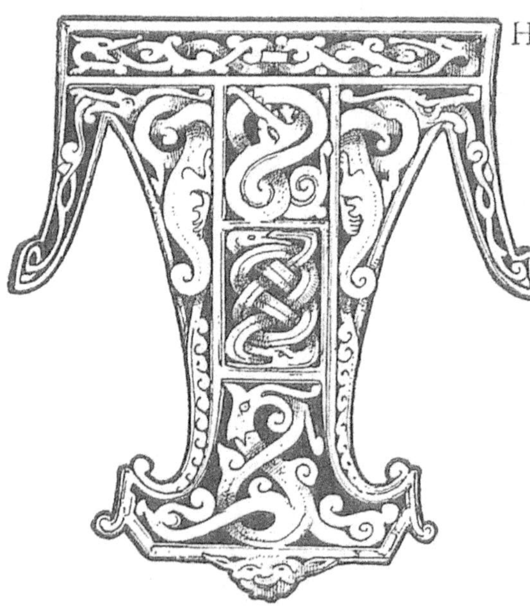

HERE is an easy kind of flat or hollow carving, if it can be so called, which is executed with a gouge or V tool, or a firmer alone, but which produces flat patterns. Make the design, and as it is to be executed almost entirely with lines or grooves, or small hollows, it must be so designed that the patterns are close fitting, or separated only by lines. Now and then, or here and there, a small corner or larger space or cavity may be removed by a touch of the tool, but as a rule there is little work in it beyond mere lines. However, as in the gouge-work of the previous lesson, although anybody can learn in a day or two to " run " the lines, yet if good patterns be available, remarkably beautiful and valuable work may be produced by it. It is as applicable to cabinets, chests, panels for chairs, or other kinds of decoration. Of course the lines, or hollows, or excavations may, as in all cases, be filled in with colour, Fig. 31.

This work can often be very well executed with the firmer (or flat carver's chisel) alone, and it will afford good practice to acquire familiarity with that greatly neg-lected tool.

Flat or cavo-cutting of this kind *as work* is only a little advance on grooving with a gouge, but its results may be very much more artistic. It occupies a position be-tween gouge grooving and cutting out the ground. Each of these are as separated as so many distinct arts, but they lead one to the other, Figs. 31-35.

The easiest way to prepare this work is to execute the pattern on

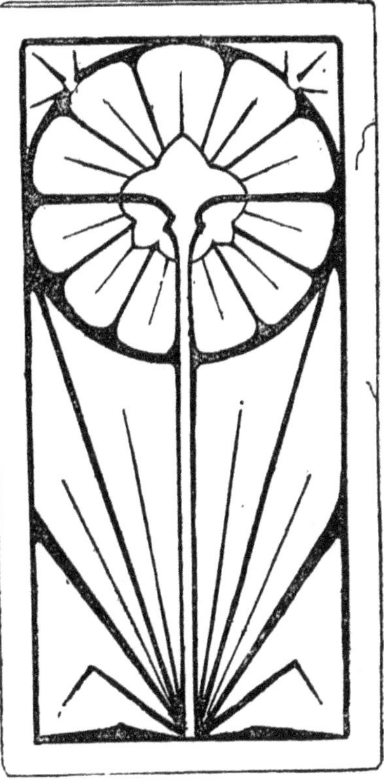

Fig. 31.

the wood in Indian ink, and then simply cut away all the black. The lines in leaves, etc., must be very carefully run with the V tool ; all the larger hollows should be cut with a gouge. If very large hollows, or spaces, or grounds are left, they must be executed as described in the next lesson.

Observe in Figs. 31 to 35 that all the carving is confined to

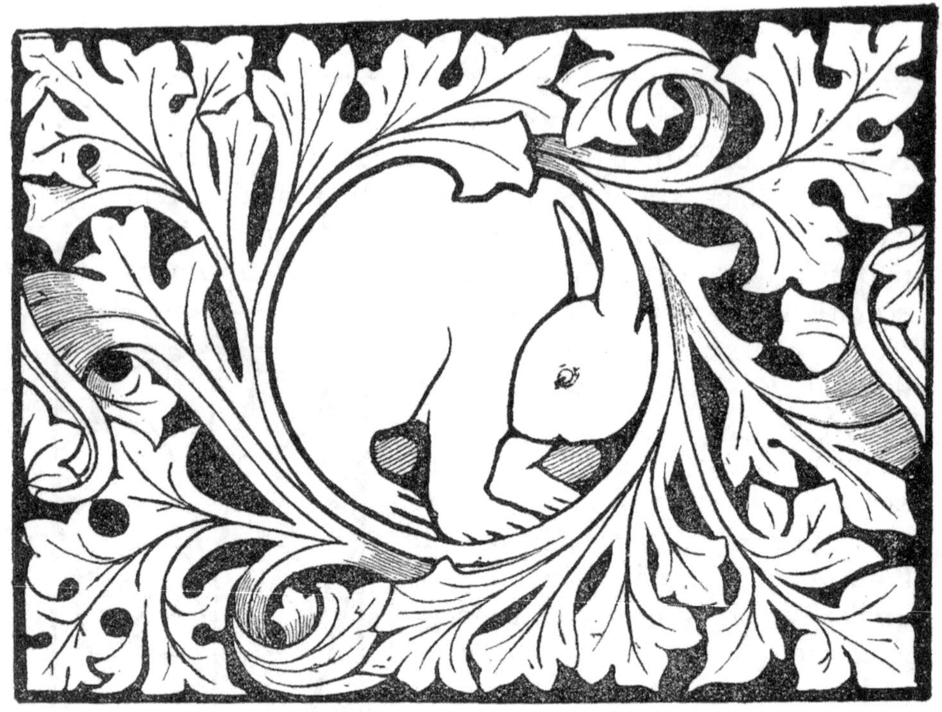

Fig. 32.

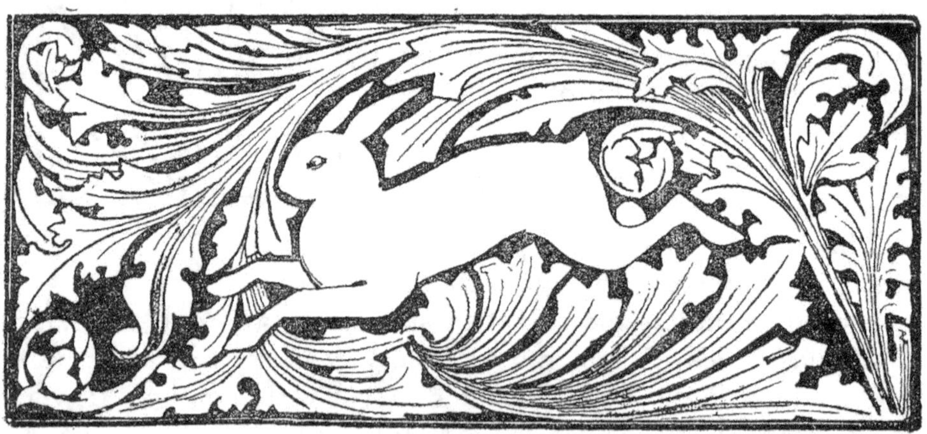

Fig. 33.
FLAT PATTERNS.

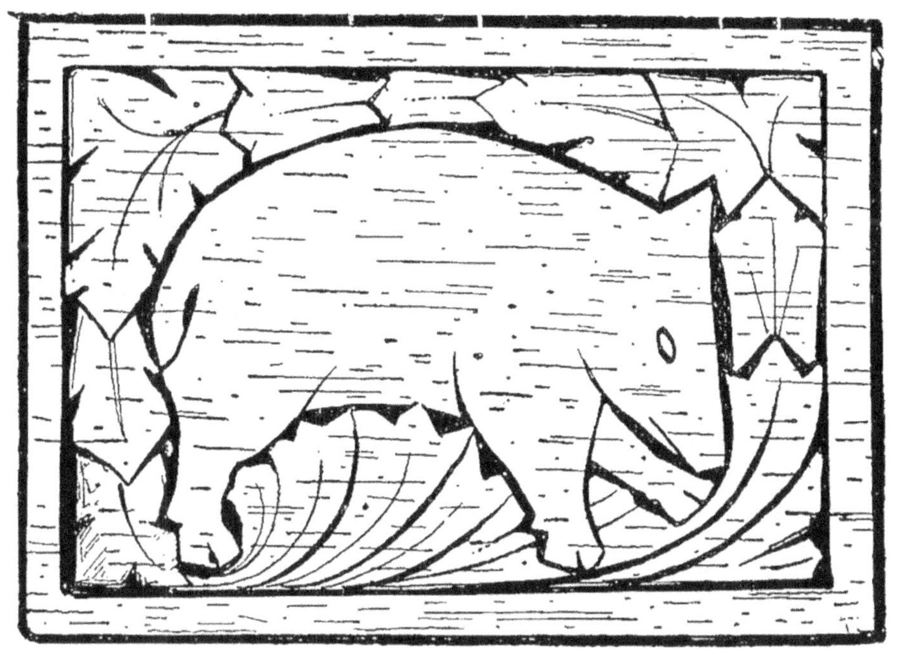

Fig. 34.

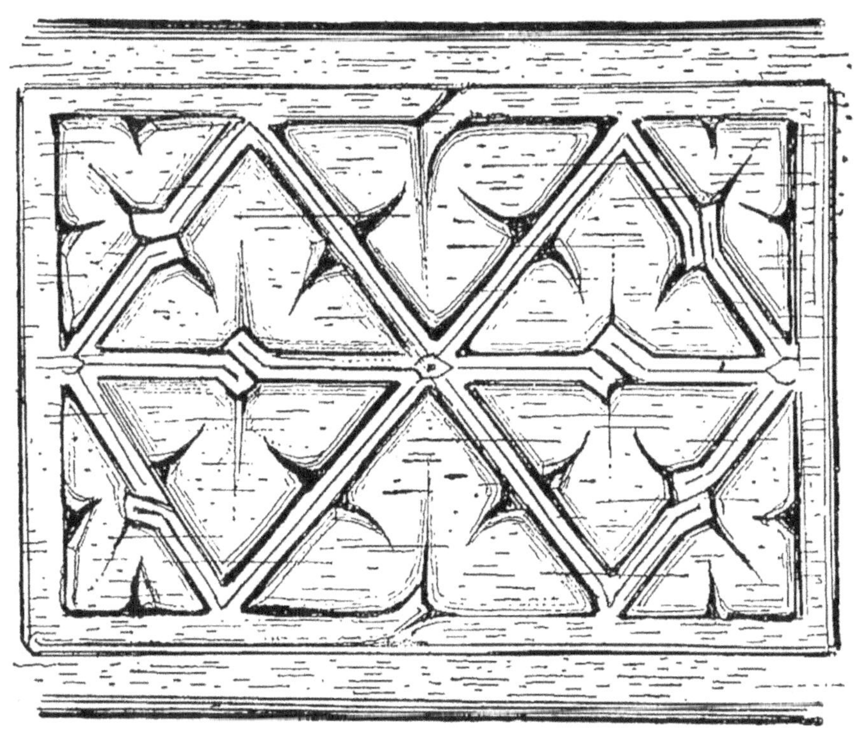

Fig. 35.
FLAT PATTERNS.

simply cutting away the parts indicated by the black ground. The fine lines can be best executed with a parting or V tool, and in many instances with the smallest gouge or veiner. Though not usual, it is excellent practice, when possible, to learn to do this with a small *firmer*, or carver's chisel.

These cavo relievo or *cut-out flat patterns* are as easy of execution as gouge-work to any one who has learned the latter. They are not now much studied, but they are capable of a wide appli-

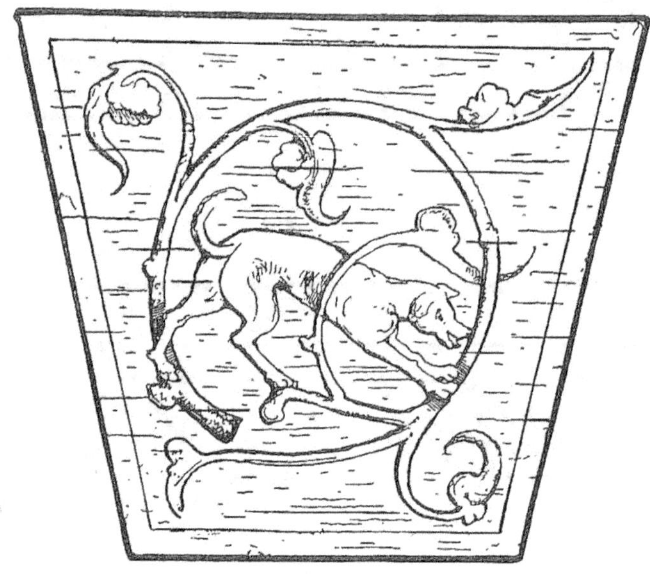

Fig. 36.

cation in large decorative art. The lines and cavities look best when painted or dyed. It is the next step beyond gouge-work, which represents simple drawing of lines in design, and corresponds to *sketching*.

Contour or rounding and modelling of course correspond to light and shade, but plain gouge and cavo-cutting is simple *sketching*. Any animal, or a human figure, a vase, flowers, or vines may be thus carved, the only further condition being that

the outlines shall always be broad and bold.   Great care should
be exercised not to make too many lines, especially fine ones,
and in all cases to avoid detail, and make the design as simple
as you can.   When in thus outlining an animal you have clearly
indicated, with as few lines as possible, what it is meant to be,
you have done enough, as in all sketching the golden rule is to
give as much representation with as little work as possible, Fig. 36.

It may be observed that familiar and extensive practice of the
very easy gouge-groove work, and of simple flat or cavo-cutting
in hollows, if carried out on a *large* scale, as for instance in wall
and door patterns, gives the pupil far more energy and confidence, and is more conducive to free-hand carving and the
sweep-cut, than the usual method of devoting much time in the
beginning to chipping elaborate leaves and other small work.
Therefore it will be well for the pupil to perfect himself in such
simple groove and hollow work.   This was the first step in
mediæval carving, and it was the proper one for general decoration.   It was in this manner that the old carvers of England and
their masters, the Flemings, taught their pupils.

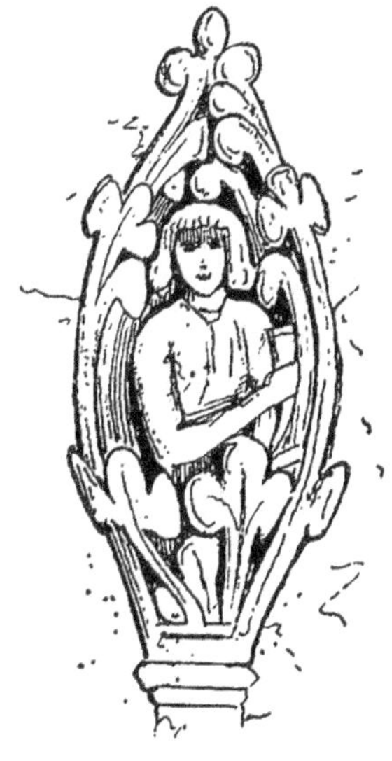

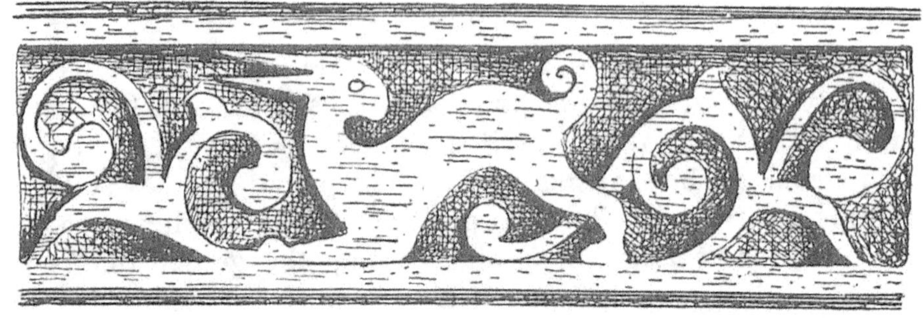

FOURTH LESSON.

CUTTING OUT A FLAT PANEL WITH A GROUND.

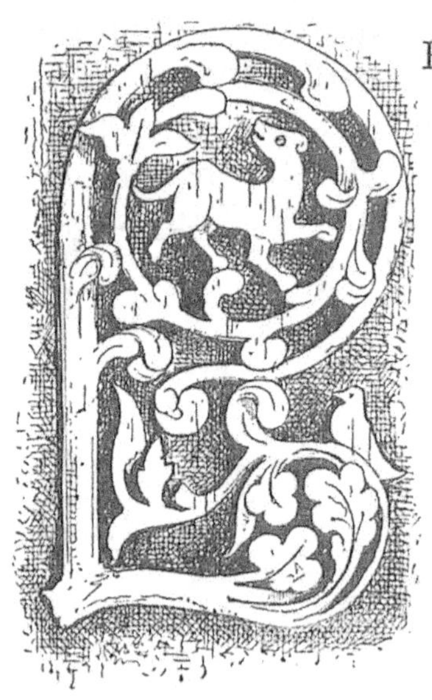

ET the pupil take a panel and draw on it a pattern, Fig. 37 *a*. He is to cut this out in what is called flat carving, and sometimes " ribbon work." He begins by *outlining*, which may be effected in different ways. I. By taking a small *fluter* or veiner, or a tooling-gouge one-tenth of an inch in diameter, and cutting a groove all around the pattern just outside of it, but accurately close to it. If perfect in Lesson II. this will be very easy for him. II. He may do this also with a V or parting tool, but the gouge is better for a *first* attempt. III. The outline cutting may be effected by taking a *firmer* or carver's chisel, one-third of an inch broad, and placing it " up and down " close to the pattern, but sloping outwardly, give it a tap with the mallet so as to sink it a very little way into the wood. Do not cut "straight up and down," but so as to make a sloping bank. IV. There is yet another way, which is more difficult and seldom practised, yet which if mastered gives great skill in carving. Take the firmer or flat chisel, and holding it with great care run it along the edge, sloping outwards, so as to cut the line accurately. By means of this method the whole work may be very well outlined. It is not urged as absolutely necessary at a first lesson, but it is advisable to practise it sooner or latter.

When the outlining is done, let the pupil take a flat gouge

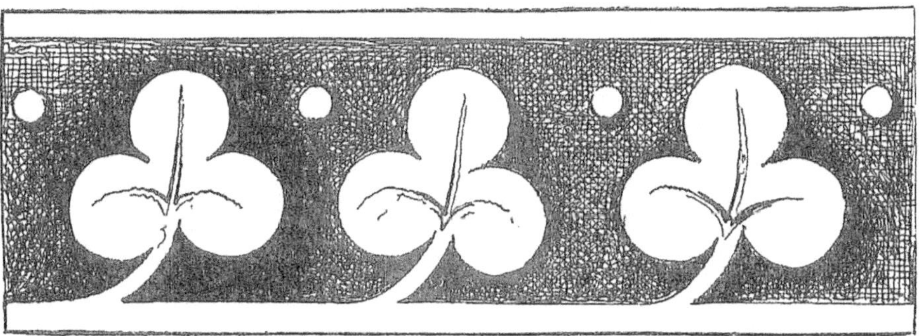

Fig. 37 *a.*

(if he has cut the line with a small gouge), and very carefully shave away the wood from the ground. Let him cut at first very little at a time, for his object is now not to make something to show, *but to learn how to manage his tools.* Do not finish all the cutting in one part at once, leaving the rest untouched, but go all over it gradually several times, until it is nearly perfect. Let every touch tell. Remove the wood at every cut, and leave no edges or splinters. To do this well you must also always watch and consider the grain of the wood at the particular spot you are operating upon ; it is easy enough to see whether you are cutting with, that is in the same direction, as the grain,

or across the grain ; but it is something beyond this that has to
be looked to. It is invariable that all wood, whether cut with
the grain or partly across the grain, will be found to work better,
smoother, and with less tendency to splinter either in the one or
the other direction, that is to say, when cut from right to left, or
the reverse, from left to right.   The required direction in which

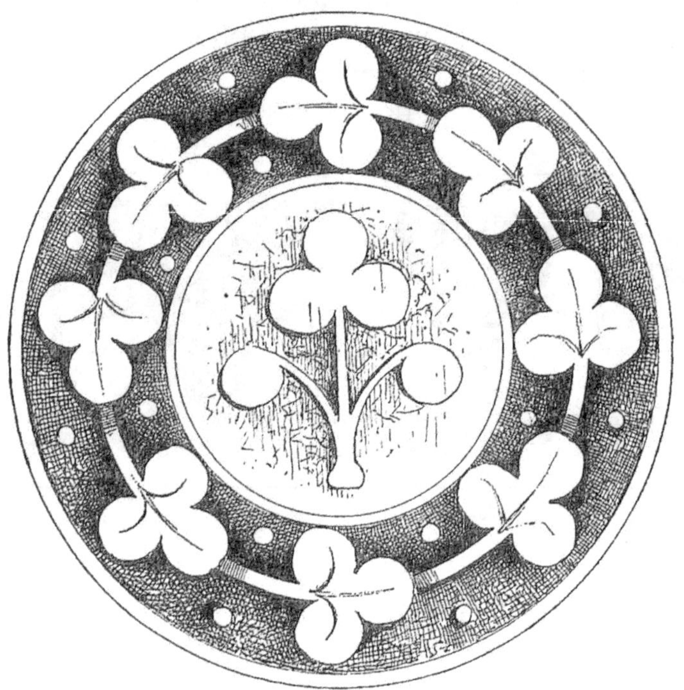

Fig. 37 *b.*

it will cut the smoothest is at once shown by the behaviour of
the wood itself and the quality of the results ; hence, should the
work or surface show a tendency to splinter, if possible cut it
from the opposite direction, and turn the work round on the
bench should that be necessary to enable you to do it, that is, if
you cannot use the tool in either hand.   Beware above all things

of letting the hands work mechanically. *Think* of what you are about. By learning to cut clean and flat you are taking the first step towards the "*sweep-cut*," which will come afterwards, and which requires both deliberation and dexterity.

When all is cut out nicely and carefully, take an extra flat gouge and clean "the floor," removing every trace of unevenness. Then take a French round nail or bodkin, and with the mallet fill the ground with little holes so as to make a rough surface ; or you may use one of the *stamps* for this. This requires care, so that the shape of the stamp may not be apparent. It is advisable to trim with a very sharp small chisel, and with great care, the edge of the pattern. For this lesson it will be best not to cut away more than one-fourth of an inch to form the ground.

If the outlining is done with a chisel and mallet, before cutting away the ground, go over the outline and cut at a little distance from the line already cut towards it, so as to remove the wood and form a V-shaped groove, as one digs with a spade.

Teachers or pupils are begged to remember that the sole object of this lesson is to learn how to handle and manage the tools ; that is, to become familiar with them, and how to learn to *cut* a ground with skill and confidence. To do this *there should be much occasional practice on bits of waste wood.* Therefore it is earnestly urged that no beginner shall go further than the work described in this lesson until he or she can execute it with accuracy and ease. When this is gained all that remains to be done is easy.

The reason why the "parting" or V tool is not specially recommended to *beginners* for outlining is, that it is the most difficult of all tools in ordinary use to sharpen. The small gouge answers every purpose for the work in hand.

To recapitulate, first, we have the cutting away from

between the outlines of the pattern : If the panel be half an inch
in thickness, it should not be more than a quarter of an inch in
depth.   Cut over the whole very lightly at first, and then go
over it again and again.   Do not dig or cut out the whole
quarter of an inch in one place at once, leaving the rest as yet
untouched.   Should you do this you will be led to cutting too
deeply in some places.   When the hard work is effectively
executed, and nearly all the wood is roughly cut away, the work
is said to be *bosted* or sketched, a word supposed to be derived
from the French *ébauché* or the Italian *abozzo*, meaning the
same thing.

After cutting Fig 37 *a*, the pupil may proceed to 37 *b*,
which is simply an amplification of the same.

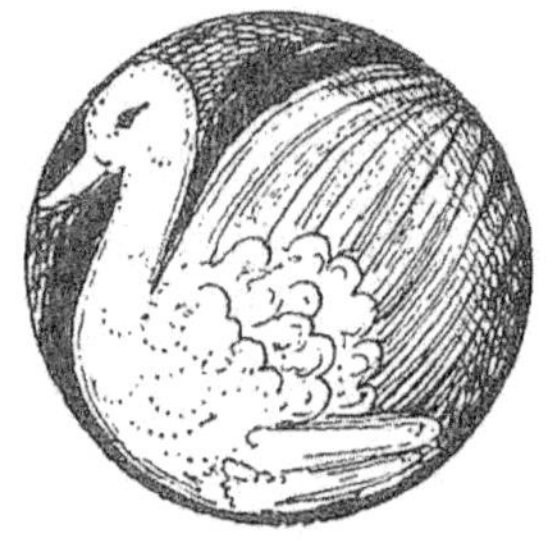

FIFTH LESSON.

CUTTING SIMPLE LEAVES—CARVING WITH THE LEFT HAND—
MODELLING OR ROUNDING—SHADED PATTERNS AND
MODELLING—PROGRESS TOWARDS RELIEF.

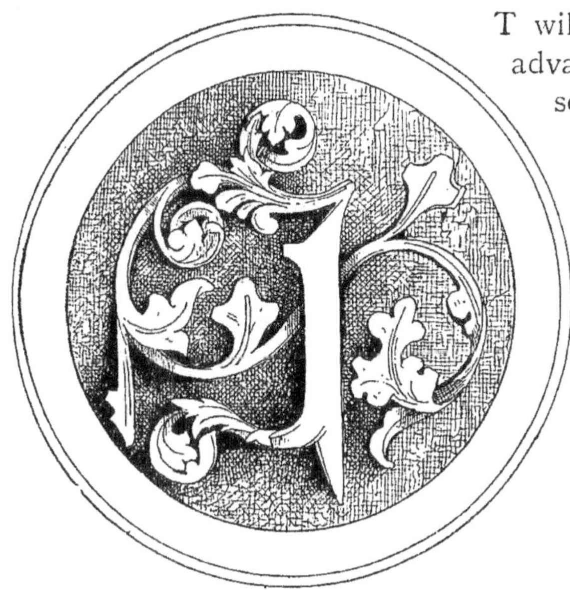

T will be very much to the advantage of the pupil, so soon as he can cut confidently and correctly with the gouge or chisel, to practise with the *left* hand as well as the right. The younger he is the easier will it be to form this habit. A carving tool is sharpened from both sides because the edge, so made, enables the artist to cut from many positions without turning the wood, and when he can use both hands he has the same advantage to a greater degree. Try, therefore, to acquire a perfect command of the tools, so as to cut with both hands, and in many directions and ways, the greatest care being always taken, however, that you do not turn the point towards yourself, lest an unwary slip should produce a wound. When you can *cut* with confidence, and do not rely under any circumstance on splitting, digging, prizing up, "wriggling," or rocking with the gouge to remove wood, then you can tell beforehand what you

are about to do. To attain this skill you must frequently
practise cutting on waste wood, and not spend all your time on
perfectly finished work.

The pupil has been instructed in Lesson IV. how to cut
out the ground from a flat panel, leaving the pattern in relief.
Very beautiful patterns may be executed with very little finish ;
and a vast proportion of beautiful old Gothic wood-carving
depended far more on outline than on modelling for its effect.
Modelling is the rounding or shaping a pattern to give it form.
Now *leaves*, in one shape or another, more or less natural, form a

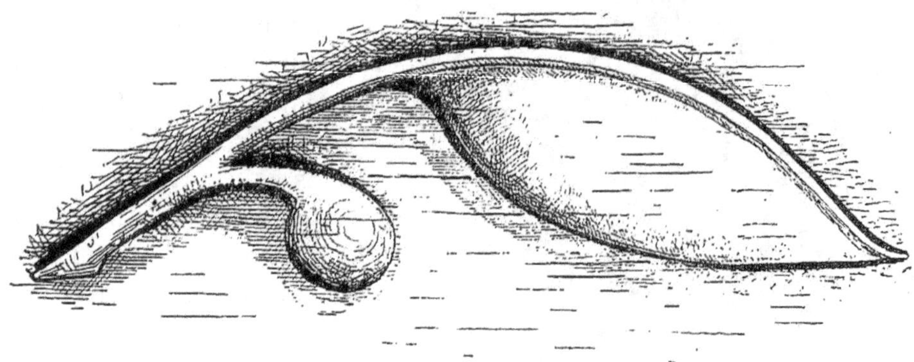

Fig. 38.

great proportion of all decorative design.   When they are sim-
plified from the original type, and made merely ornamental, yet
still preserving so much of the original shape that we can plainly
see what that type was, they are said to be " conventionalized."
It is, therefore, very important that the wood-carver should
know how to carve leaves well.   He has already learned how
to make the simple outline or groove of one or many with a
gouge, and how to remove the wood surrounding them.   He
may now go a step further and cut with great care the elementary pattern, Fig. 38.   Use a flat gouge for gradually rounding
and carving the surface, beginning with the outer or lower edge,

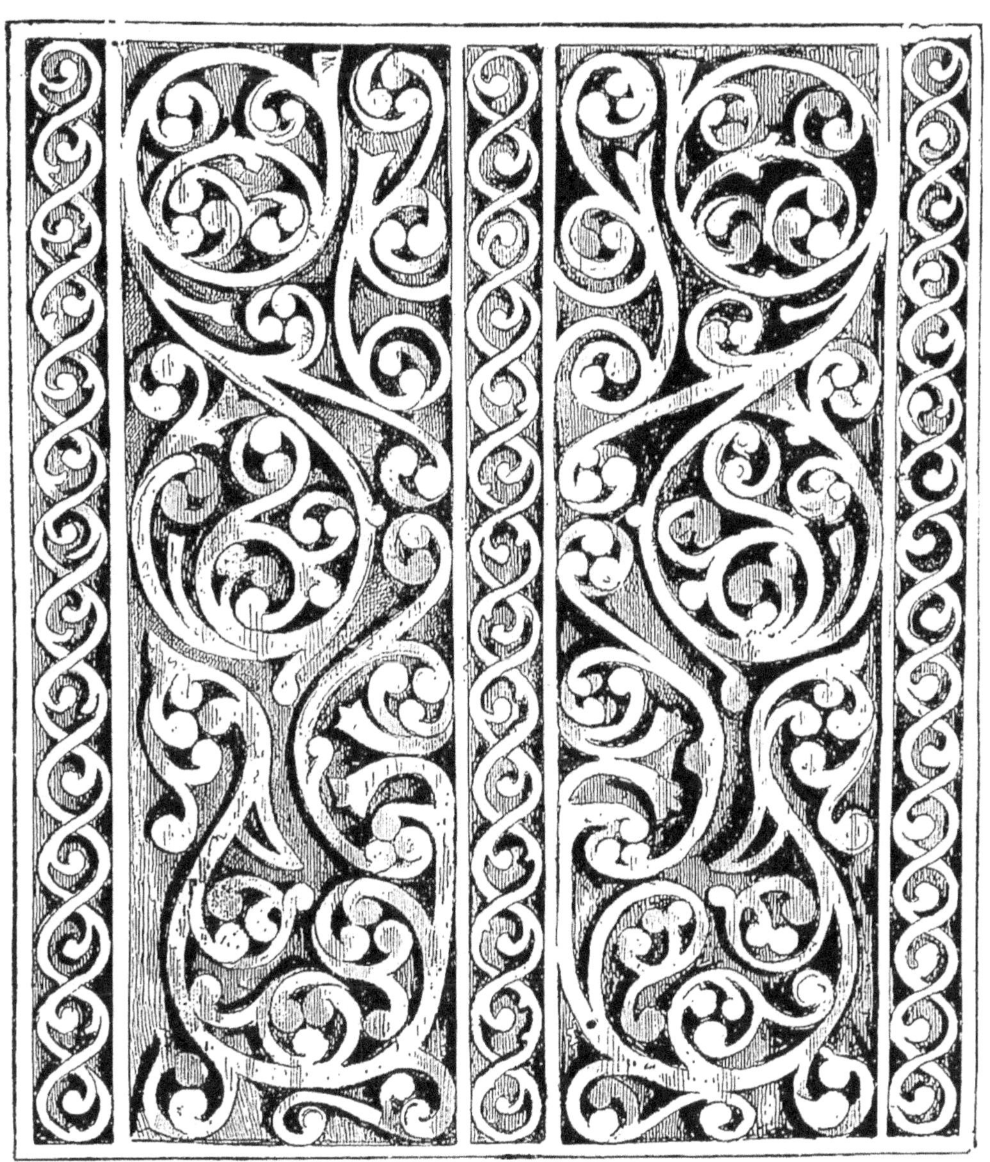

Fig. 38.

and working up to the stem. The pupil will do this as well
again, and with far greater confidence and ease, should he begin

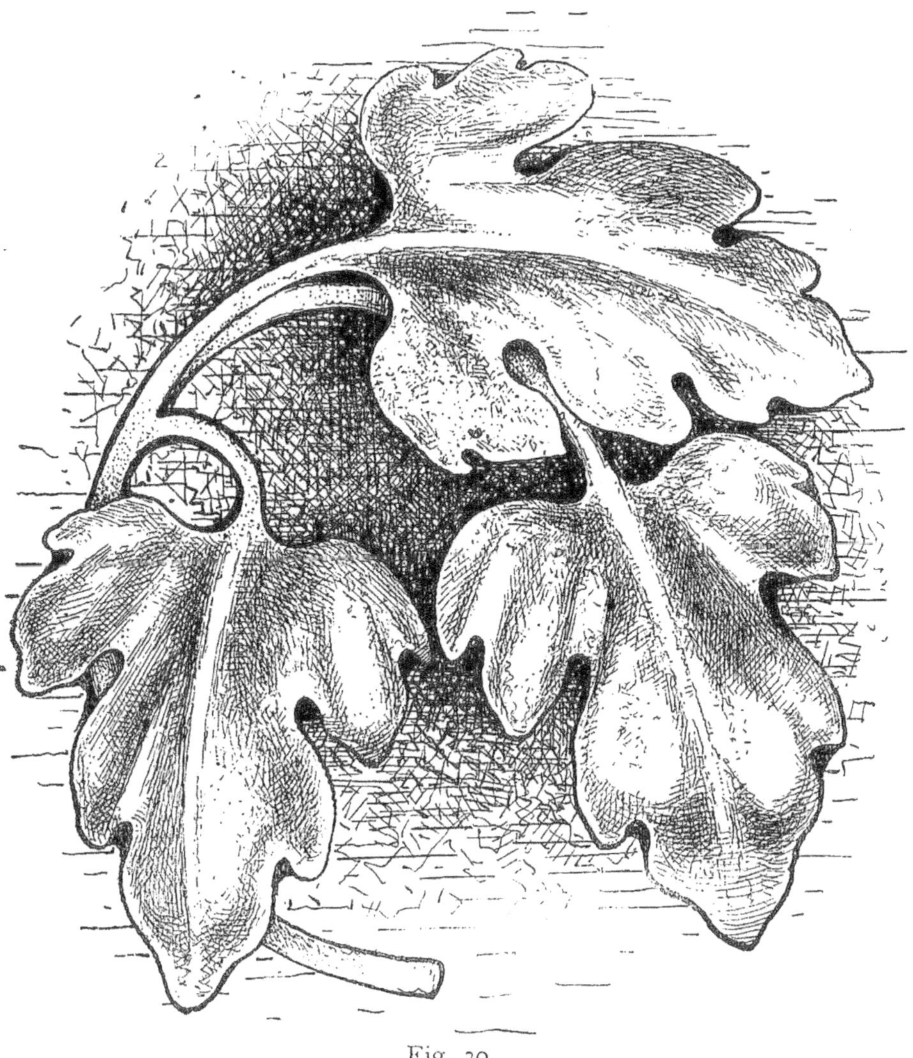

Fig. 39.

firstly by making a shaded copy of a leaf in pencil, then modelling it in clay, and then copying this in wood. The time thus

spent will be gained in the end many times over by the skill and dexterity and eye-training acquired.

The first step in rounding a leaf is effected simply by "wasting" or chipping away little by little by straightforward cutting. This is the same for convexities and hollows. Such rounding and undulation is performed by skilled artists with very few tools, including gouges, skew-chisels, rasps, files, and the double-bent gouge.

The student may, in the beginning, round and scoop his leaves with any tools which seem fit, if he will only cut with the utmost caution, and keep the implements well sharpened. A very important and rather difficult part of this work is the cutting the ribs or stems which run through the leaf. One implement for this purpose is the so-called "macaroni tool," but at present it is really very little used, owing to the great difficulty of keeping it sharp, and its liability to break. Nearly all veining can be executed with the fluter or large veiner, the hollow gouge, the V tool, or the flat gouge, according to circumstances.

"The wood," as Eleanor Rowe remarks, "should be taken off in short, sharp touches, and not by deep and long cuts, and no attempt should be made to obtain a smooth surface until the form and general modelling of the leaf is done." The edge of the leaf may be a little under-cut to give relief; this effect should be given by a V tool or small veiner. When the leaf is correct in form, proceed with flat gouges to remove the tool marks, holding the tool very firmly, and inclining it to an angle of about 45°.

It is advisable for the beginner to cut several simple leaves with great care, Fig. 39, and, if possible, let him draw, shade carefully, and model them all in clay before carving them. He will be astonished to find how much easier the latter process is, and with what confidence it can be carried out, after the two former have been executed. Having for several years had under my supervision large classes in wood-carving, both with and without modelling in clay, I speak from experience on this subject.

It is to be observed that, as leaves and sprays involve every possible curve, he who can design, model, and carve them well, will find no difficulty in executing birds, animals, or the human face or figure. In their simplest forms, or in flat work, these are all extremely easy. Then they may be a little rounded, or modelled, and so going on, step by step, the carver may come to full relief. Oak leaves are, perhaps, the most graceful of all objects, and lend themselves to as many forms as the acanthus, but they are also very difficult in their more advanced developments. Therefore they form an admirable subject for study.

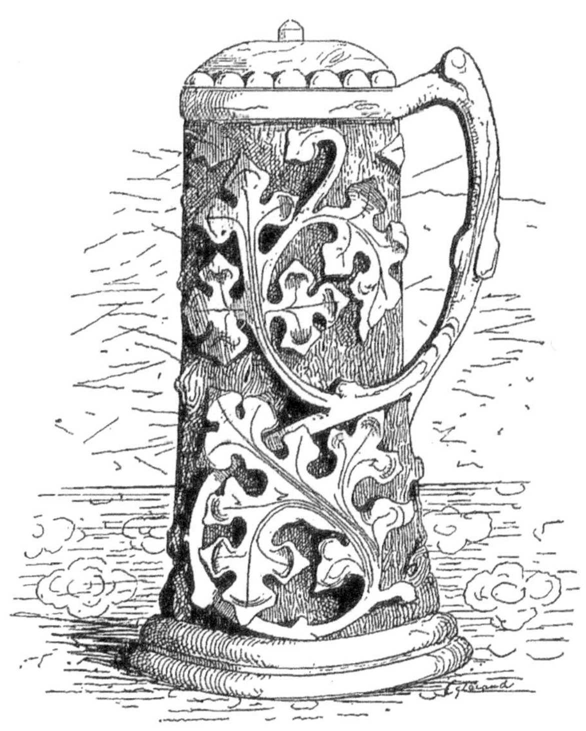

SIXTH LESSON.

CUTTING WITH THE GRAIN—TURNING THE TOOL—THE DRILL—BOLD CARVING—AND LARGE WORK.

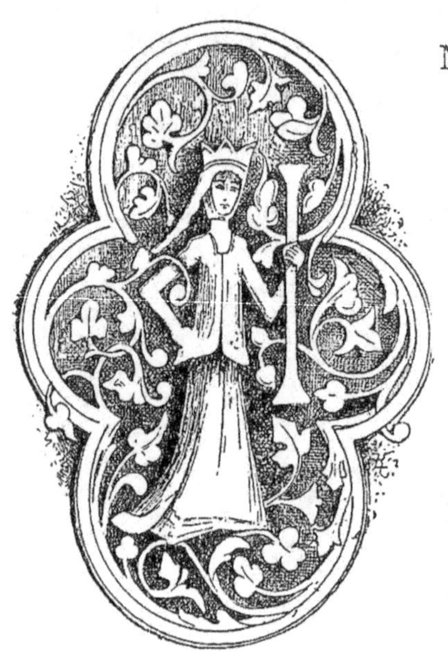

N both large and small carving there is one common difficulty, the frequent resistance of the grain of the wood and defects incidental to it. This question has already been touched upon in the Fourth Lesson, where the pupil has been told that he will usually find the wood cut more readily from the one side towards the other. To this may be added, that as he progresses and carves in higher relief he will not only find the same thing in working leaves and other ornament, but he will also find that some portions about these will always cut better, more smoothly, and without splintering, when the tool cuts downwards, that is, from the surface towards the background, but with other and quite adjacent portions when the tool is made to cut the reverse way or upwards. As a first rule, therefore, so soon as there is the smallest sign of splintering, try the cut from an opposite direction to remove it, and it should cease.

Further, if the edge of the gouge or firmer cut in certain directions *against* the grain of the wood, it will "catch," or tear, or splinter. As another precaution against this, the carver may shift the position of the wood by unscrewing it, if it is held by a clamp or holdfast. This is more easily effected if he have, in

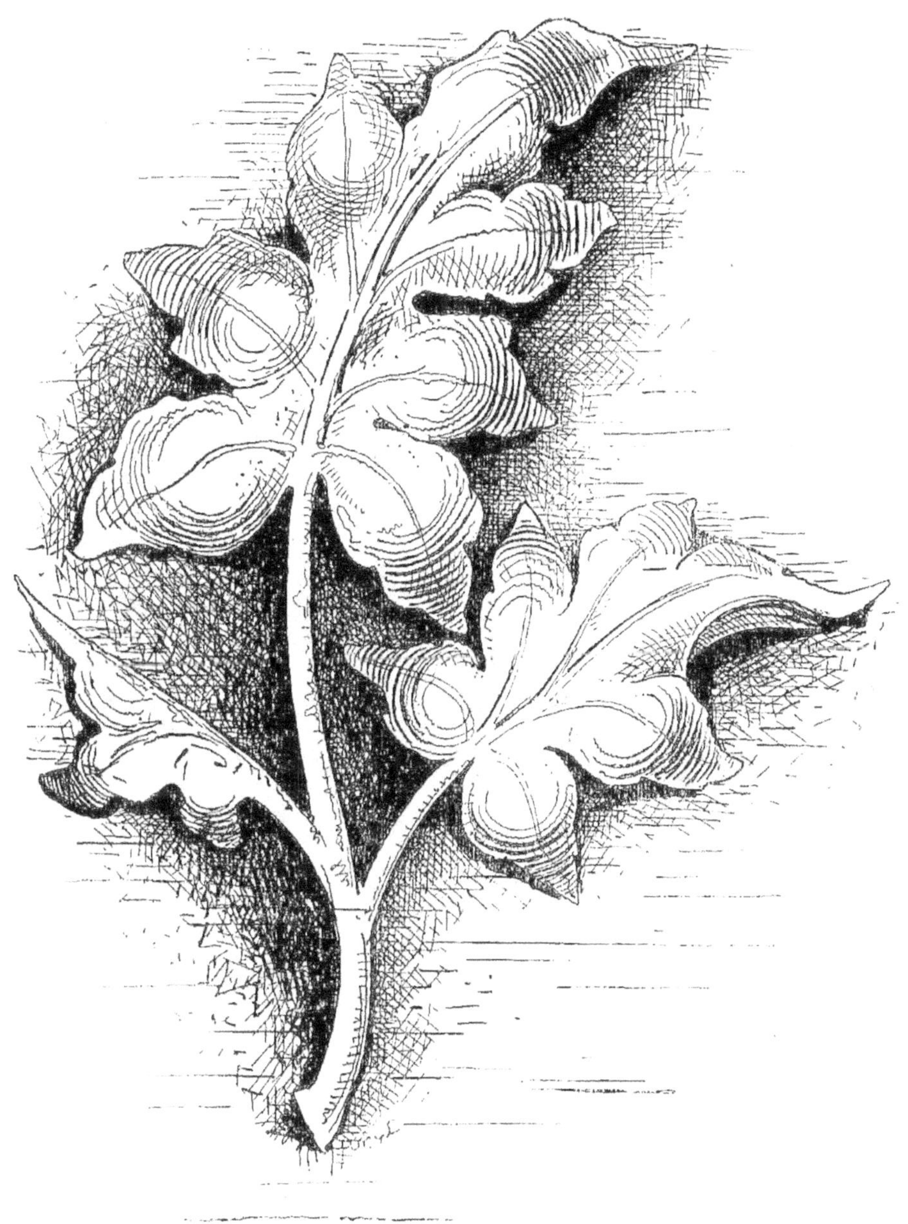

Fig. 40.

the French fashion, only three or four nails driven into the table, in which case he has only to pick his work up and put it into a different position ; or he may shift his own position. But it is

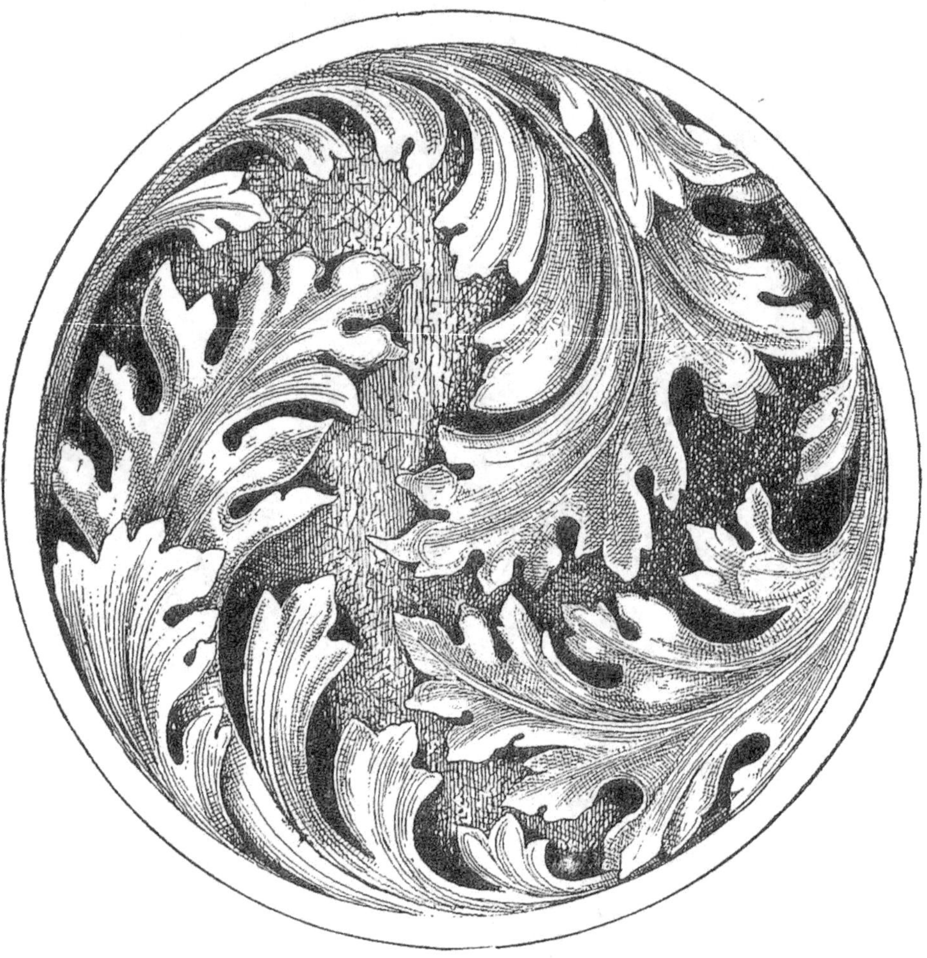

Fig. 41.

best of all to be able to carve with both hands, a feat which, after all, is not difficult to acquire, and which comes very soon with a little practice ; and to master the art of *turning the tool about and cutting in any position,* which also comes with practice to an incredible extent. He who can do this, can manage to cut with the grain in most cases without shifting the block.

Wood should *never* be torn or ripped ; everything should be done by clean, smooth cutting. To make sure of this you must first of all keep every tool as sharp as a razor all the time, and always cut with the grain. Cutting diagonally, or partly across, is still cutting with the grain, and is easier and surer than going parallel with it.

Mark out the pattern, Figs. 40 or 41, and outline it. The Greek and Roman workmen, and very often those of later but early times, with a gimlet, or drill, or centre-bit, bored out holes here and there, both in wood-carving and in stone, and worked up to, or around these. They formed beginnings, as it were, to guide the gouge or chisel. These were often of great practical utility wherever a small round cavity occurred, but their chief use in wood was to aid and direct the tool in certain places where there were difficulties of grain to contend with, or sharp points or corners of ornaments likely to be broken off. I was once puzzled to know why the drill was so much more used in ancient than in modern carving, but reflection convinced me that where decorative work must be done expeditiously or cheaply, and a little coarseness of execution did not signify, it was a very great aid.

In the pattern, Fig. 38, the leaf is easy to cut ; that is to say, one single leaf. Cutting it once more, or repeating it, is only doing the same work over again ; yet if this same leaf, or another not a bit more difficult, be repeated twenty-five or thirty times in a wreath, it will seem to be a very difficult piece of work. Now, it is a matter of importance to understand that if you can do a very small, simple piece of wood-carving really well, you can also by mere patience and repetition execute a piece of work which would seem to be very remarkable, or quite beyond your power. The illustration to this lesson, Fig. 40, shows what I mean. Almost any one with care could cut out a leaf, and he who has done one can *repeat* it in any other arrangement. Now a vast proportion of all decorative patterns in flat or ribbon-work, and even in higher relief, are formed on this principle of repetition, or of so-called "lobes," so that he who can carve even a little neatly may be confident almost from the beginning of being able to execute even valuable work.

Such a panel as Fig. 41, when once carved, may serve for the lid or sides of a box, the cover of an album, or any object with a smooth, flat surface. But I cannot repeat too often this injunction, to constantly practise cutting on waste wood, so as to acquire facility of hand, before attempting anything which is to be shown or sold. It is unfortunately true that, left to himself or herself, there is not a pupil in a thousand who would not devote all the time or work to producing show-pieces, even at the first cutting, instead of practising so as to learn how to produce them.

When pupils have teachers who are practical and workmanlike, it is probable that as soon as they can handle the tools they will be set at *bold, large work*. This is fortunate for them, since it is the greatest advantage one can have, be it in Design, Modelling, Wood-carving, or any other art of the kind, to be made familiar with free-hand, large, and vigorous execution.

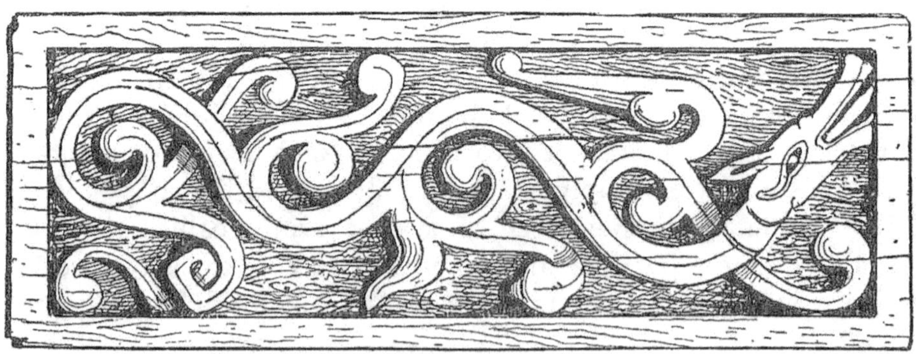

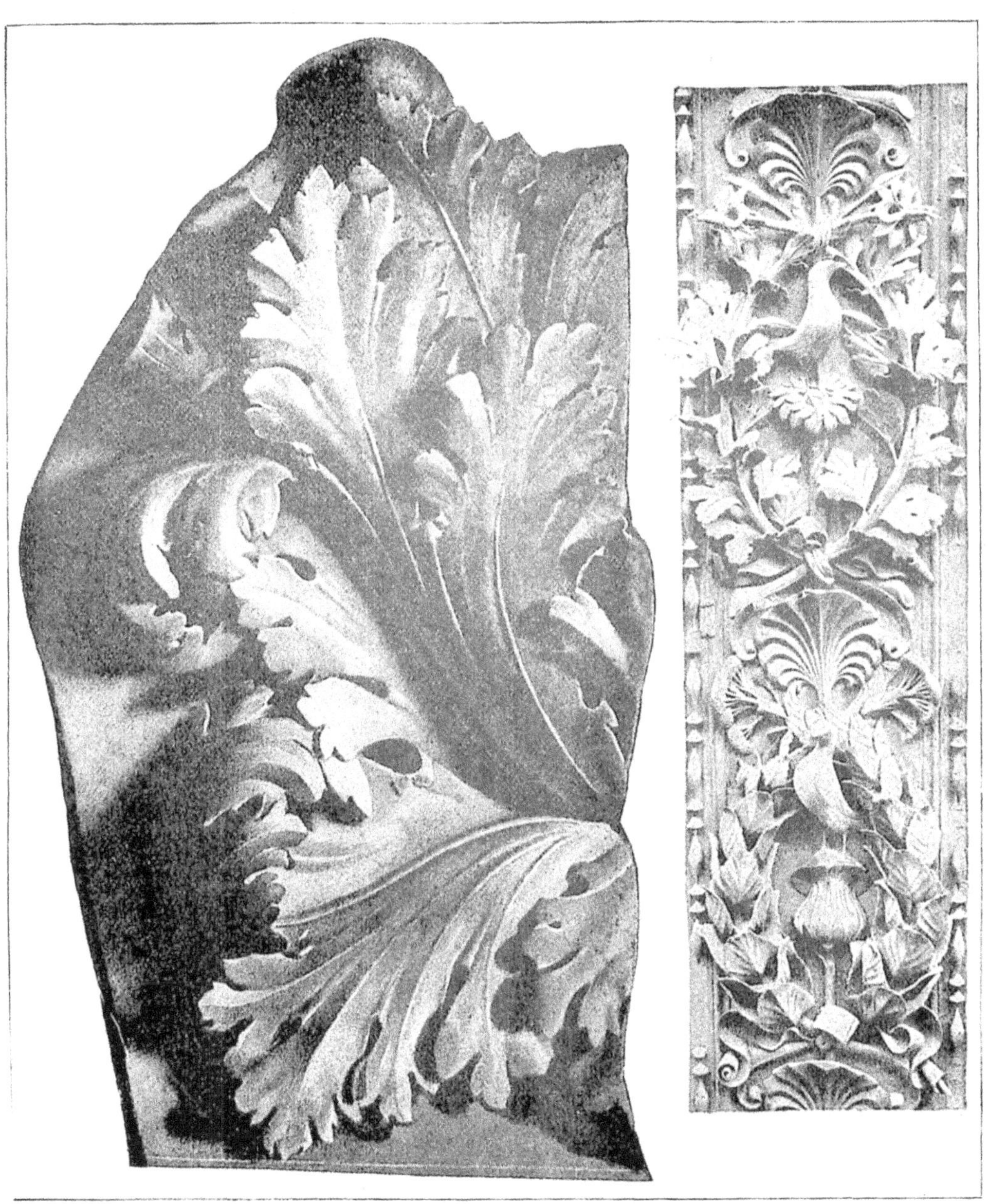

HIGHLY FINISHED STUDIES OF FOLIAGE.

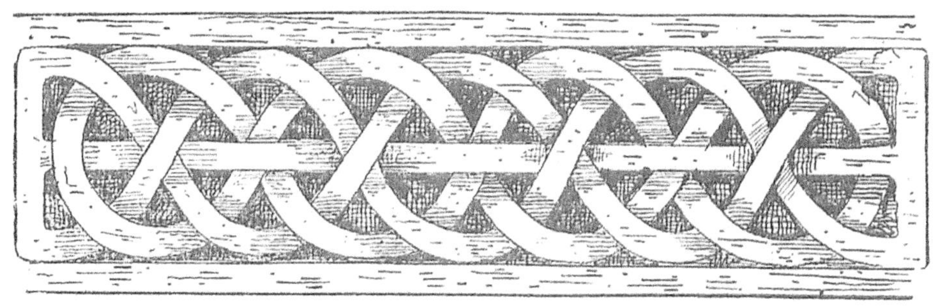

SEVENTH LESSON.

THE SWEEP-CUT OR FREE-HAND CARVING—CUTTING
NOTCHES IN LEAVES—THE ROUND-CUT.

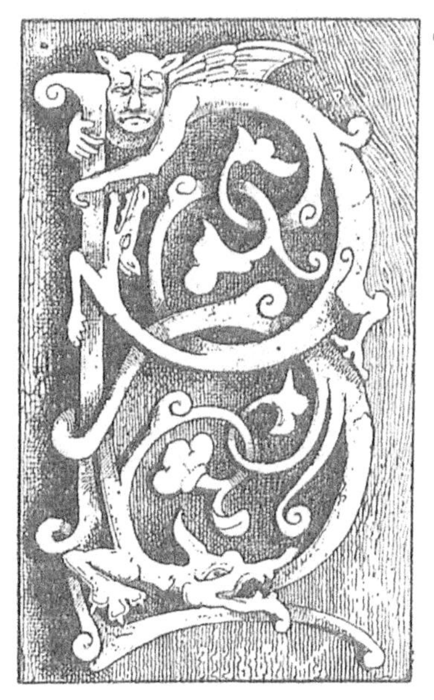

OLDNESS in cutting is a matter of very great importance, since no one can carve really well till he gets beyond chipping or " wasting." To carve boldy we must use the sweep-cut. It may be observed that in modelling in clay there are certain methods of shaping the material, which are quite peculiar; as, for instance, when we press the modelling tool down or up, and at the same time turn it to the left or right. This makes an inclination upwards or a depression downwards, yet sloping to one side or the other. It is made by two movements in one; so in cutting with a sword or long knife, if we chop, yet at the same instant *draw* the blade, the result is a much deeper incision. This is called the draw-cut, and by means of it a man may cut a sheep in two, or sever a handkerchief or lace veil thrown into the air.

Very much like this is the double motion of the hand in the *sweep-cut*, which must be acquired by all who would learn to carve leaves well. It is not quite true that all work must go through the three stages of blocking out, bosting, and finishing; for when leaves are carved with the sweep-cut they are generally finished at one operation. With this cut, which is usually performed with a flat gouge, the wood is removed so as to give a peculiar form or curve—as when a leaf slopes down and sideways—by a single but compound movement; that is, we must, while pressing the edge, also move it or give it a slight lateral motion. This sweep or side-cut is developed more fully in sloping larger and especially rounded surfaces, like

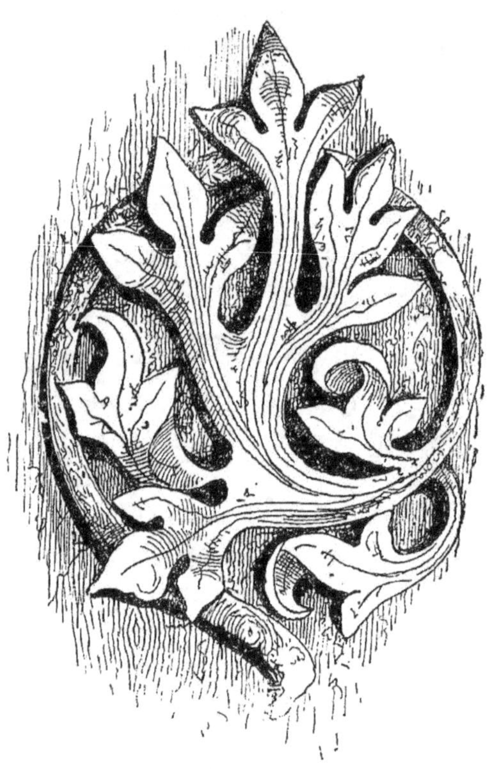

Fig. 42.

whole leaves, which rise and fall, or undulate, Figs. 41, 42. This cut, by means of which one can carve with confidence the most brittle and difficult wood, requires a tool of very good quality, which must be kept scrupulously sharp. It must be practised on waste wood till the pupil is a master of it, but when it is once acquired, wood-carving, as regards all large and effective work, may be said to really have no further difficulties. With some it seems to come all at once, by inspiration.

The simplest or first form of the sweep-cut occurs in making leaves. Every one who has tried this knows that the cutting the notches or making lobes in the wood, but especially the shaping the points, is a difficult matter, for if we simply shove or press the edge of the cutter, as in ordinary or *plane* work, the leaf will probably break, especially if the wood be "splitty," uneven, or brittle. Having marked out a circle to include the lobes of the leaf, we cut a notch half way between the proposed points, and by shaving first from one side and then the other, bring the leaf or its lobes into shape, Fig. 43. Of course, in doing this we cut *from* the point to the corners.

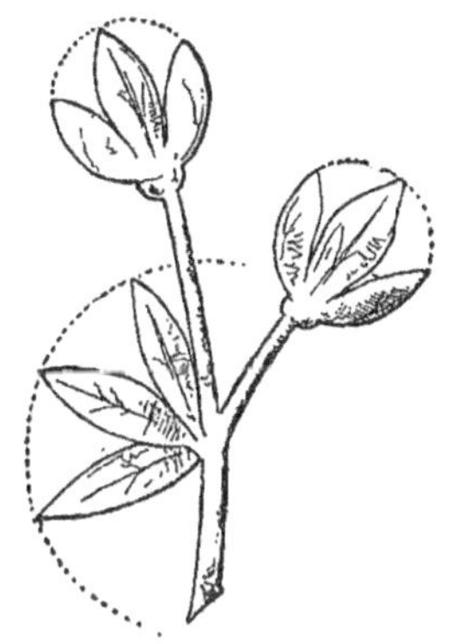

Fig. 43.

For the present it will suffice to apply it in its simplest and easiest form to cutting groups of leaves. In the previous lesson the pupil has been told how to cut out a single plain leaf in relief by simply "wasting" or chipping away the wood little by little with a flat gouge. In like manner it might be filed, or rasped, or scraped like metal, into shape. Let the pupil now sketch Fig. 43, and then bost it out, by cutting round and clearing away as already described.

The dotted lines indicate the original shape or circles in which the leaves are cut. When it is "all done but the finishing," or bosted, then cut the notches backwards in the manner already described. And, as I have said, if the pupil has practised the sweep-cut, and keeps his flat gouge perfectly sharp, he may cut the finest notches in the smallest leaves in the splittiest wood without once breaking away a piece.

The sweep-cut gives perfect confidence, and he who has acquired it, and knows how to apply it so as to make any curve or boss or involution which he pleases, may be said to have passed from the amateur stage to that of the artist, or at least of the clever workman. By means of it one can model the most refractory wood into any shape, and to any one who is expert at it oak is as easy to carve as pine. Therefore the pupil should spare no pains to acquire it; and it will come sooner perhaps than he expects if he first of all takes all pains to understand what it really is, and secondly to practise it for a few hours on waste wood. There are, however, many carvers who pass months or years in "wasting" away wood by simple straight cutting or chipping before they get any idea of what a sweep-cut is—if indeed they ever learn it. But if the pupil has previously acquired skill, that is to say, ease and confidence in running gouge lines and hollow cutting and shaping simple leaves by straight cutting, he will without doubt find that the free-hand sweep-cut comes as by inspiration.

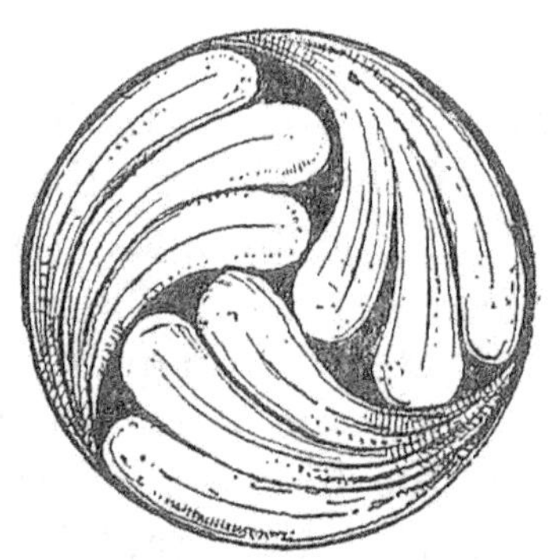

EIGHTH LESSON.

FURTHER APPLICATION OF THE SWEEP-CUT TO HIGHER RELIEF.

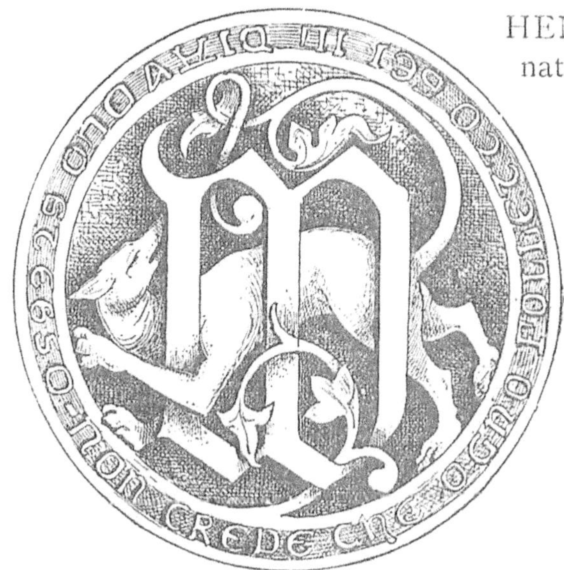

HEN a leaf is in its ordinary natural condition it is generally flat, but while growing or fading it often curls and twists into remarkable and graceful shapes, which are extensively employed in decoration. Before going further I would impress it on the intelligent student that the mere literal imitation of any kind of leaf, so that it would look exactly like a *real* leaf if it were only coloured, should seldom or never enter within the province of wood-carving as a general decorative art.

What the pupil should do in copying leaves and flowers, etc., or in modelling them for carving, is to observe their characteristic shape and contour, to follow all their graceful lines and bends, depressions and swellings, and give the general expression and spirit of these without striving *too* accurately to make a mere leaf. He should not make it so thin that it would break with a slight blow. A great deal of the most admired work of the present day is of this kind, which will hardly bear dusting.

A leaf may always be cut, as we see it done in classical and in ancient work, so solidly and firmly as to resist the wear and tear of centuries. As nobody is expected to believe that it is a real leaf when it is palpably cut out of wood or stone, we may as well conventionalize it (that is, keep only a general likeness to a leaf), and make it attractive by grace and skilful combination. And this can be done if we only cut out the leaf in its *general* form and leave a strong base for it to rest on, so that it may be

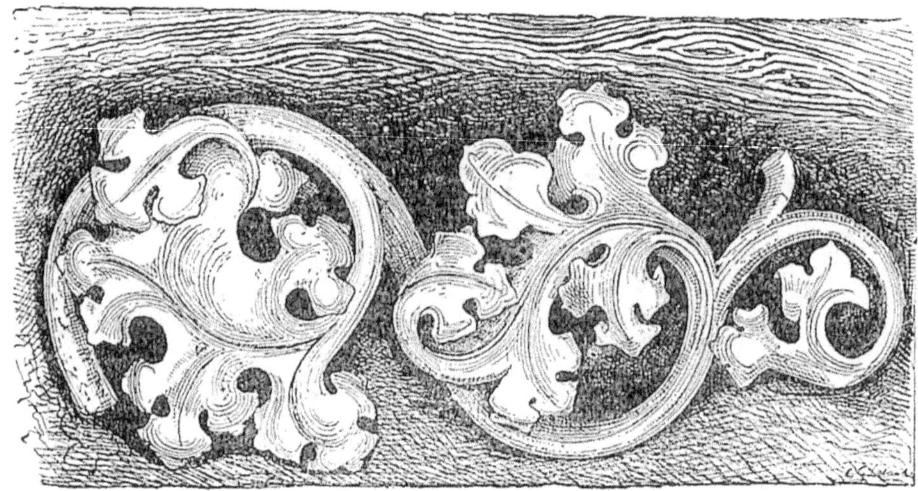

Fig. 44.

safely dusted or rubbed against. The student should try to understand this, for it will enable him to make all effects necessary in decorative work, and save him much needless petty labour.

If the pupil has practised the sweep-cut, and can with confidence work in any direction, with both hands, he may now attempt oak-leaves in which there are varied slopes, cavities, and swellings, Figs. 44 and 45. These seem to have been the favourite subjects of the old modellers and carvers. Perhaps the best designing of the kind in existence is that by Adam Kraft, in Nuremberg. I repeat here, that the more difficult and varied a leaf is the more necessity is there for the pupil to model it in clay, or at least to draw and shade it carefully, before beginning. The reason is this, that, having its principal points in the memory, it is much easier to reproduce them when cutting in wood; we know then when and where to turn the hand or the tool. And it is well to bear in mind that this practical and necessarily accurate, though often hasty, sketching and shading of the workshop grows very rapidly on the pupil, so that, being driven to it, he learns to do such drawing more promptly and vigorously than he would in a school or class.

In making the sweep-cut it is necessary *to get the bend* or movement, which is directing the gouge in the proper route. In ordinary cutting we only push the blade forward; in the sweep-cut there is a "draw" or side movement as well as a push. But the *bend* or direction constitutes, so to speak, a third movement, and this is the most difficult to determine. To get a certain symmetrical turn or curve we cut *without seeing*, whereas in ordinary cutting or "wasting" we see clearly just what we are going to slice off, and take it away with confidence. But with a little practice on waste wood, the sweep or draw-cut will become so familiar that one can execute the most difficult curves, not by chipping away, but by a bold sweep. Amateurs who have taught themselves can generally cut or chip only straightforwards; they cannot turn or curve a leaf with a sweep. The combined movement given to the tool in making the sweep-cut may be thus analyzed, and if the three distinct forces applied to the tool be first understood and then kept in mind in making such cuts, success will soon and easily result. Suppose we are engaged upon the surface of a leaf which slopes generally downwards and off to one side, but also has a rise or mound somewhere in the course of the slope, and most leaves have one or more such undulations. With the gouge, straight or bent, grasped firmly in the right hand, and the two fingers of the left hand pressed on the surface *and side* of the blade about an inch from the cutting edge—the position already described : the tool is pushed straight forward for the entire length of the cut by the right hand ; at the same time the blade is pushed to the right or pulled to the left by the two fingers of the left hand to the extent, and as the slope may travel to the right or the left ; and thirdly, the right wrist is raised or lowered to cause the tool to travel over the intended mounds or undulations on the leaf. Now these three distinct movements or forces exerted on the tool merge into one another, and may be said to be used simultaneously, and are really one continuous movement, which gives the sweep-cut ; but the extent to which any one preponderates of course depends upon the particular shape of the leaf or scroll being carved, and is soon found out by but little practice upon different forms.

In commencing or bosting out this pattern, Fig. 44, and all others in high relief, the pupil will do well to observe that he should select a gouge whose sweep will fit the curve of the leaf in the part it is intended to begin upon, and placing the edge of the gouge outside, but quite close to the line, and holding the tool at a slope so as to cut away from it outwards, give it a moderate blow with the mallet. Take care not to drive the gouge in too deeply. This is the *blocking out* of the leaf, or outlining in the solid. And in doing this, begin by making or cutting the general outline only. Leave the second-sized interstices or hollows for a second cutting, and the smaller notches of the leaves and fine corners for a final finishing. In this pattern, Fig. 44, also Figs. 42 and 45, the leaves should be of the natural size, or from three to five inches in length.

Most beginners cut too closely under the leaf, so as to get at once to relief, which looks like finish. As a rule it is better,

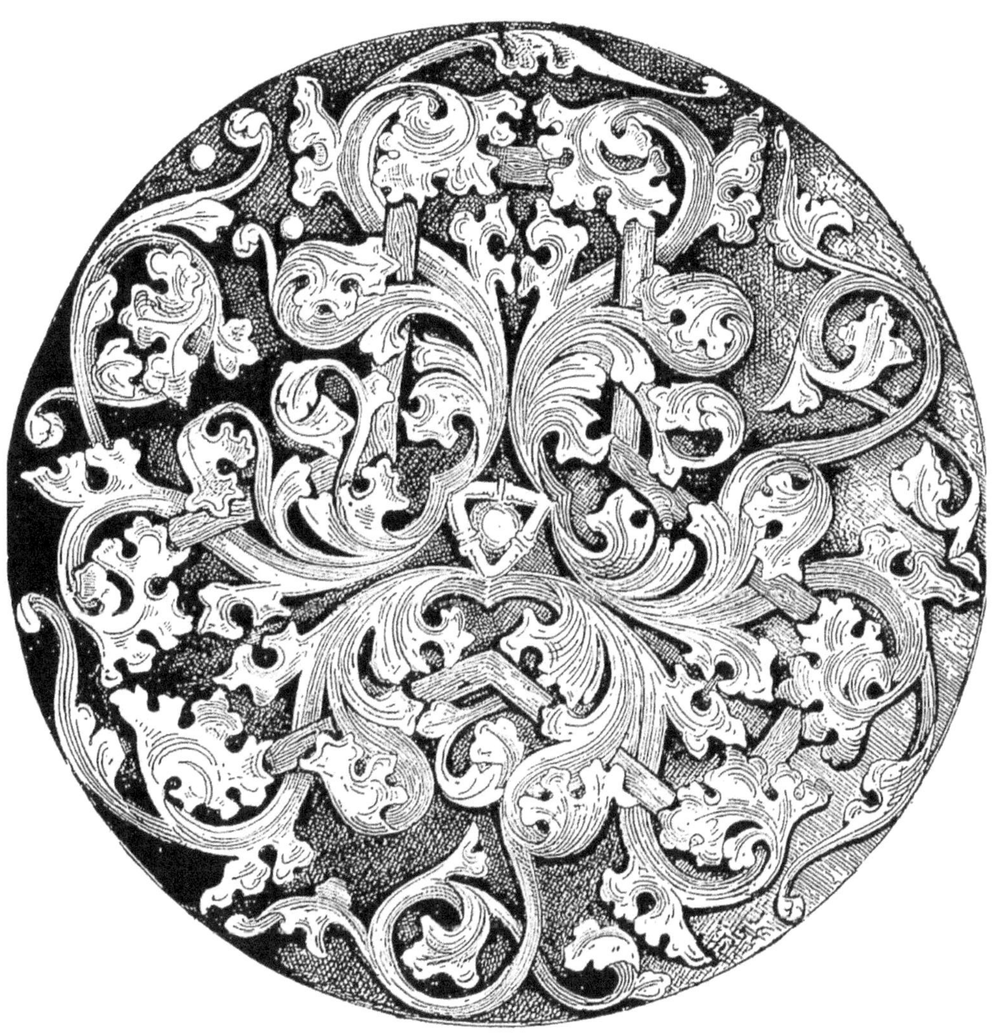

Fig. 45.

CIRCULAR PANEL IN HIGHER RELIEF.

whatever the pattern be, in flat ribbon-work or high relief, to always rather slant outwards. For in the first place, when we come to finish in ribbon-work, the pupil may find it necessary to cut so much away to bevel or round or undercut the pattern, that (especially when it is in narrow lines) the *thinning* away will quite destroy their proportions. But it is well on yet another account to be very sparing of this paring away and undercutting. There are far too many wood-carvers who cut away under in order to make leaves thin and natural, till they are like paper, and much more fragile. This is greatly admired as indicating "skill," and it certainly demands skill of a common order to effect. But it requires a much higher and nobler kind of *art* and will to make the leaves strong and firm, even if we conventionalize them—so that their curves are really beautiful. And this may be done, and at the same time all the most beautiful and characteristic features of leaves be preserved.

In ribbon or flat carving, a strong shadow or relief may be got as follows. In cutting, slant the chisel or gouge outwards at an angle of 45°, thus /. When the grounding is finished, cut under the slope, half way up. The outline will then be like a <. This sharp edge may be cut away a very little, such as ⸦, or even into a rounded ⸦, in which case there will be a marked line of shadow all round the edge.

Having blocked out the whole quasi-perpendicularly, that is, in one direction or on one side, proceed to cut away the most apparent hollows or depressions. With care and measurement even the beginner will soon find his leaves beginning to assume shape. If he has not learned as yet to cut and sweep boldly, he may finish the whole by simply wasting the wood away with straight cutting, aided by the file, riffler, or rasp. In fact, for many beginners, and especially for those who are slow to learn, this straight cutting and rasping is really advisable, because it at least makes them familiar with handling tools, and teaches

them how to model and hollow out. Beginners always experience great dread or hesitation as regards hollowing and
curving "in the round," but when they perceive that an object
is beginning to assume shape they take heart, and when they
have succeeded with one or two by easy, certain work, even with
the help of rasps, they will carve with more confidence.

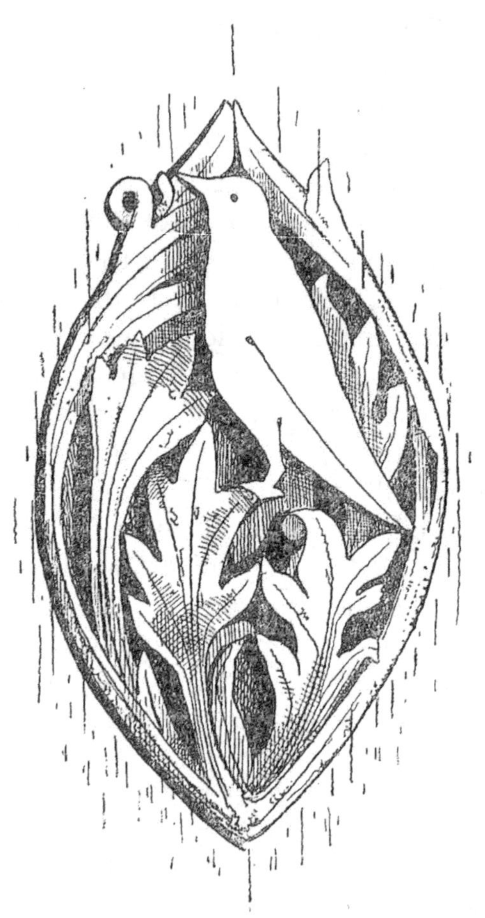

ORNAMENT FROM THE DUOMO, FLORENCE.

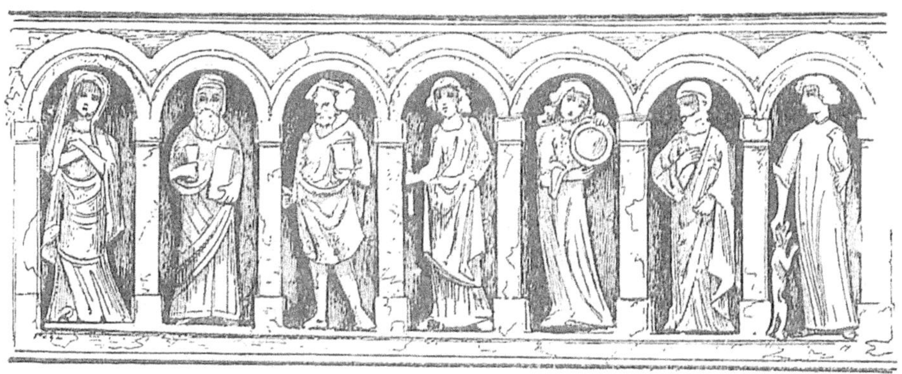

NINTH LESSON.

CARVING SIMPLE FIGURES OR ANIMAL FORMS—FIGURINI
FOR CABINETS—SIMPLE ROUNDED EDGES AND
APPROACH TO MODELLING.

HEN the pupil has had some practice in carving leaves and similar ornaments in relief, he soon learns to deepen or to cut them higher and higher, and then to model them into form. He may now, if he chooses, attempt some simple animal forms. A bird, a duck, or a hare hanging up, will present no special difficulty to him, firstly, if he will obtain one of Swiss work, already carved in wood, and imitate it. There are few towns where he cannot obtain something of the kind. It is true that much Swiss wood-carving is not at all to be recommended as regards style or finish, but it will do very well for a beginning. The best method would of course be to model a hare in clay after a dead one. In any case he can make a beginning by buying some toy animals, carved in wood and not painted. These are made by being sawn or turned out of wood into the profile section. This is then sliced into many pieces and each of

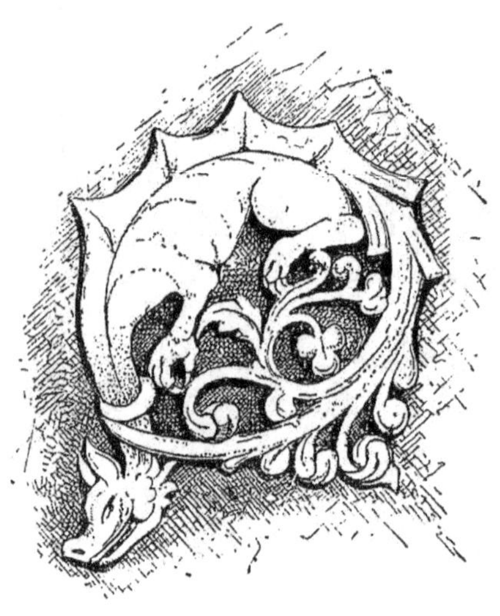

Fig. 46.

these carved, sometimes fairly well, into an animal. The wool or hair is imitated in the very small gouges or V tools, and sometimes scraped with a rasp, comb, or other tool. After the blocking out such work presents no peculiar difficulty.

The process is quite as easy as regards the ordinary or grotesque animals in Gothic carving. Draw such an animal, Fig. 46 or 48 *a* or *b*, and having fairly bosted it out, proceed to very gradually round away the edges. If it be, for instance, a serpent, which is everywhere round, this process is very simple, especially if after the cutting we smooth it with files and glass-paper. It will shape itself. Now the limbs of animals, and even of human beings in low relief, may be rounded in this manner to approximate correctness; or to correctness enough for initial ornamental processes. As the pupil proceeds, and improves in modelling and advances to copying—let us say excellent patterns of Renaissance and classic work—he will go far beyond such beginning. But there is in itself absolutely no reason why, if he only draws his outlines correctly, he should not begin by this simple Gothic work.

Whatever a pupil can draw from life or a block, *that* he can shadow ; and whatever he can draw and shadow he can model (or *vice versâ*) ; and whatever he can model, he can execute in wood ; nor would the working it out in sheet brass or leather

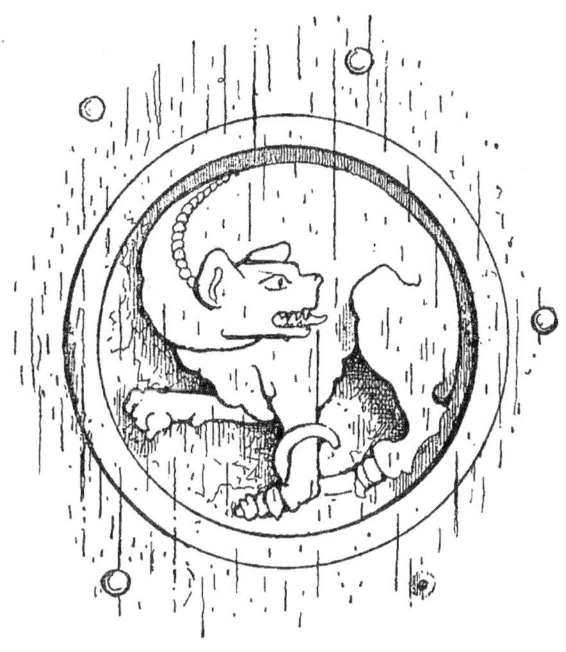

Fig. 47.

trouble him at all. This is the best way to work, so much the best that, under all circumstances, and in spite of all drawbacks, every wood-carver should strive with all his heart to learn to draw and model ; for in so doing he will learn a great deal more than all three of these cuts put together, for he will most assuredly have acquired a faculty which will help him in anything which he may undertake.

Having learned to sketch out, bost, and round simple figures,

I advise the pupil to execute a number of them, with or without leaves and ornaments. He may thus sketch and cut fishes, animals of all kinds, human figures in outline, until he feels a certain confidence and ease as regards their execution.

What the pupil must do, therefore, in this lesson, is to draw, bost out, and round easy animal forms. At this stage let him pay more attention to the few points which constitute general correctness in a sketch than to minor details. I refer to the

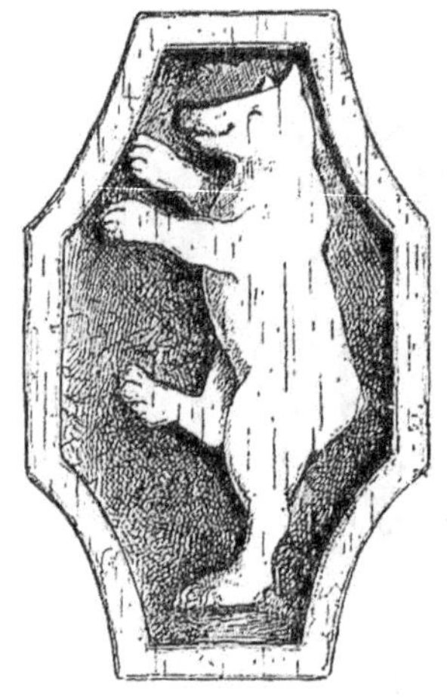

Fig. 48 *a.*

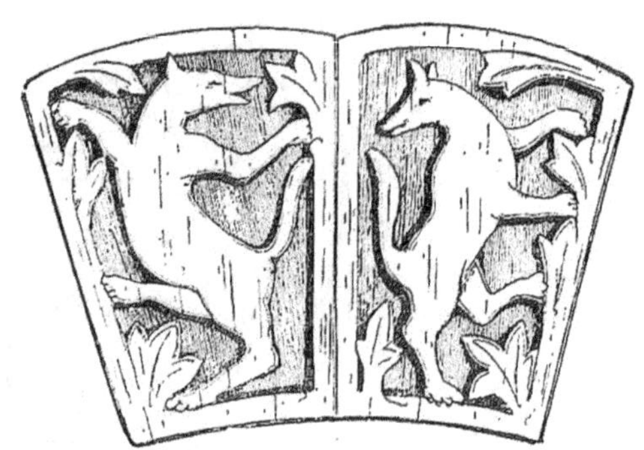

Fig. 48 *b.*

general distances of the eyes, joints, outlines of legs and back in a horse, deer, hog, etc.

Simple figures may be executed in flat or ribbon-work, or in the lowest relief, as well as in any other work.

The Italian carvers, for cabinet making, in the fifteenth and sixteenth centuries, made great use of *figurini*, Fig. 49, also the ornament on page 60. These were little statues, generally of human beings, from three to five inches in length. They were, in ordinary work, rather sketched out than elaborately carved, but the effect was good ; sometimes a hundred of them would be worked into a single cabinet. These *figurini* were also very freely used in later Roman and Roman Byzantine stone and ivory work, generally as rows of saints or scriptural personages, every one filling a niche under a round arch. These latter were often as rudely and simply shaped as it is possible to conceive, yet, owing to their " making up " or disposition, as subordinate parts they were in good taste. Any carver with a little practice can produce them. Rows of *figurini* in niches were frequently used for borders, or to surround caskets.

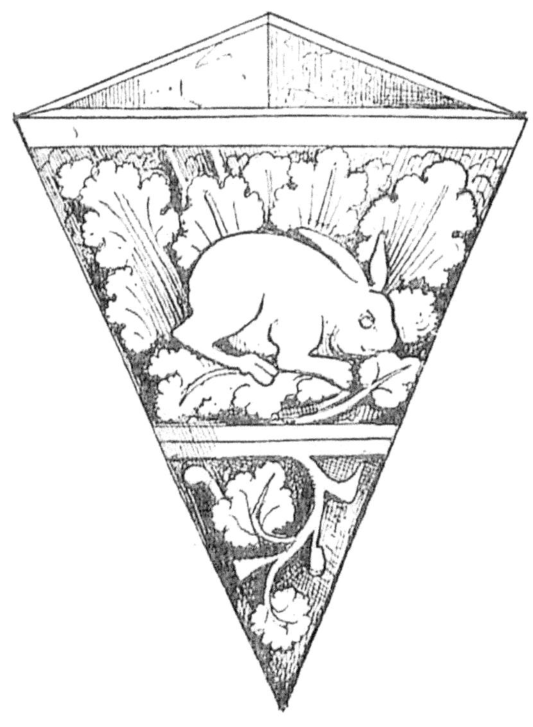

HANGING BOX FOR A CORNER.

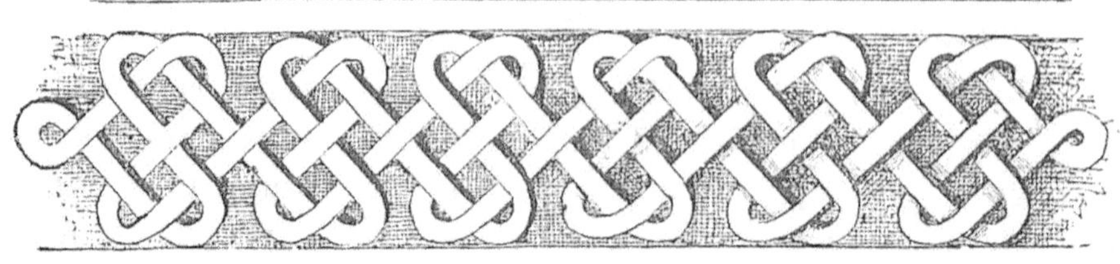

TENTH LESSON.

FINISHING OFF—IMITATION OF OLD AND WORN WORK—
WHERE POLISHING IS REQUIRED.

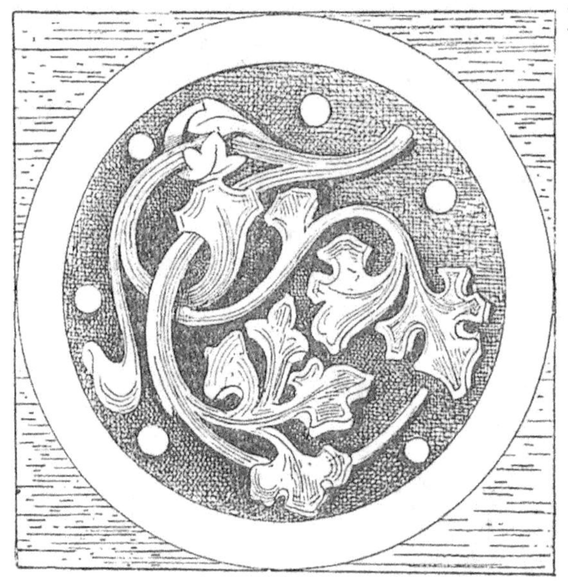

HE finishing off of wood-carving depends on what the work in hand may be. If it is a piece of carefully executed foliage, or leaves (and leaves, like *crochets* in decorative art, is a term widely applied to all shooting out or growing ornaments), it is of course the best plan to finish only with the gouge or chisel, so that the skill of the artist in clean cutting may be evident. But it has become the fashion for writers on wood-carving to insist on it, as a law without exception, that all wood-carving must be finished by cutting ; that glass-paper and files should on no account be used, and that a carver should not seek to smooth over the surface of his carving, as if to conceal how his work has been executed. In wood-carving, as in everything

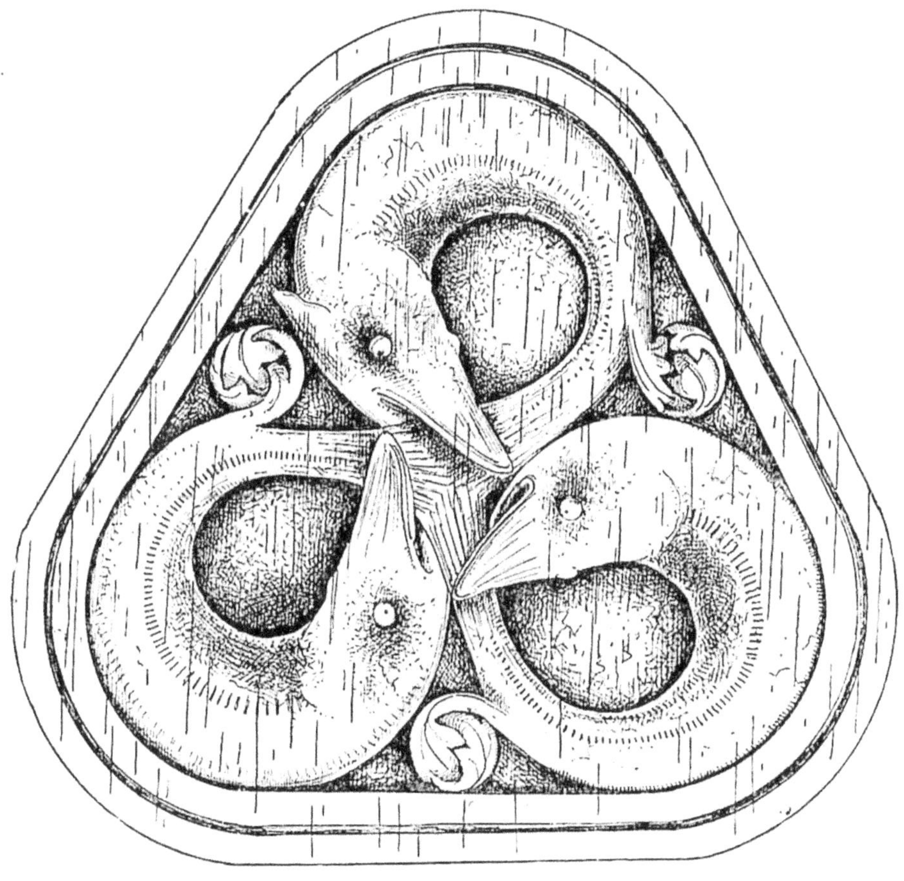

Fig. 49.

else, a true artist does not go by mere rule. He uses what tools he pleases, and finishes as he pleases. He does not confine his work to a single kind, and declare that everything should be limited to that in which he or certain experts excel. An examination of the beautiful and curious wood-carving in the great hall in Venice will convince any one that other things as well as leaves may be carved in wood; and that when these represent, for instance, old books with metal clasps, or household utensils, or arms, imitation may be legitimately carried so far as to polish the surface. Again, it may very often occur to the artist to imitate old and worn objects, such as a pilgrim's bottle, a casket or horn, for age in this way often gives very beautiful and curious effects of light and shadow, polish or roughness, differing very much and very advantageously from the stereotyped uniformity of style of too many schools. All of this requires a wide departure from the no-polish theory.

The truth is that the beginner should indeed *learn* to cut clean and well, and to do all his work with an edge, without files or glass-paper, but there is no law why he should go no further. A great deal of the beauty of many old objects comes from a certain worn look, by which they have lost some crude defects. We will now consider how such polish may be given.

Draw on a panel half an inch thick, more or less, Fig. 49. Having bosted it out, *very* slightly undercut the figure, not completely, but by rounding the edge a little. Do this firstly with the chisel, as neatly as possible; then take files. For many places in your work, especially for smoothing grounds where the work is difficult and the curved tool not available, a bent file is most useful, and these may be had of every shape and curve. For rough finishing you may use rasps and large rifflers, for finer work small files. Having brought your work into shape, you may scrape the ground flat with pieces of broken glass or a tool made for the purpose, or a chisel. Then take glass or glass-paper, the former being greatly preferable, and with care finish still more. It may now be advisable to oil all the carving, if oil is to be applied. Lay the oil on with a broad flat brush, but if there are any places which it will not reach, use a smaller paint or camel's hair pencil. Let the oil soak in for a few days in a warm room. Then with a piece of very soft pine wood, rub with great care. The harder you rub the better the polish will be, but also the greater the risk of bending or indenting the surface of the carving ; therefore great care is necessary. The longer this polishing is continued the better the effect will be. Workmen often spend as much time in polishing a piece of work intended to be handled as it took to carve it.

It may be observed that in using the glass-paper it is often very difficult to get into certain holes or cavities. These are reached either by making a bit of the paper into a roll, or by folding or rolling it around the end of a stick cut for the purpose. But the most effective way of all is to take a stick, say of the size of a lead pencil, or according to the cavity, round the end with a gouge and glass-paper, dip the end into glue, and, while it is moist, into powdered glass. When dry these make admirable finishers, and they can be again dipped when the glass begins to wear off. Glass may in this manner be put on the ends of old bent files.

When there are figures of animals, or leaves, or bands intended to be thus finished and polished *all'antico*, or to resemble worn work, it is not advisable to put in them too much inside work or *in-lines*. Inside work is, for instance, the feathers on a bird, the hair on an animal, the scales on a fish, the middle lines and veins of leaves. A very few lines to serve as indications must suffice. But the student of old and time-worn carving cannot fail to draw all these conclusions for himself.

The last finish to be given to such work may be executed by rubbing with the hand. This communicates to certain kinds of wood and other substances a peculiar polish, which nothing else can really give.

In a very large proportion of simple flat or ribbon-work the effect is very much increased or improved by polishing the pattern, and leaving the ground rough or indenting it.   This is not only perfectly legitimate, but commonly done in marble or metal *repoussé* of every kind, as well as leather-work, and yet every writer on wood-carving repeats as a duty the injunction that there must be " no polishing," and nothing but cutting.   This is, indeed, equivalent to prohibiting the application of wood-carving to furniture, objects to be handled, house and many other kinds of decoration.   But, in fact, there are instances in decoration in which paint or dyes, French polish, nails or other metal work, may be most artistically and beautifully combined with wood-carving, as many thousands of relics of the Middle Ages and Renaissance prove.

Polishing a pattern makes it shine, while roughing or dotting a surface darkens it.   Therefore, when we want in decoration bold effects of light and shade, we may legitimately polish the parts which are in relief.   Elaborately cut work which is to be studied by itself in detail, and not simply as a part of a whole, need not be polished or rough ; its finish will depend on the conditions of its design.

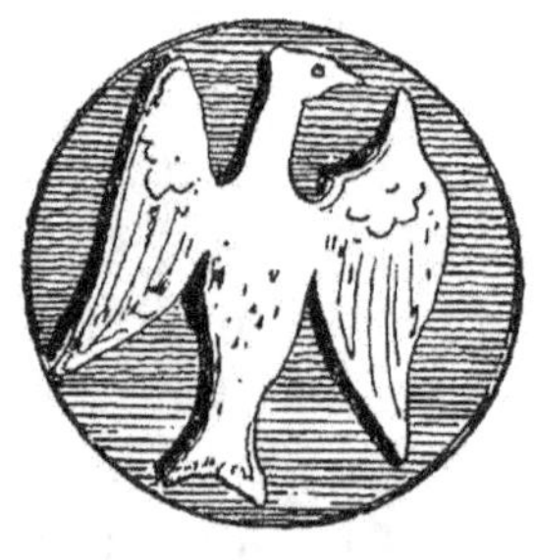

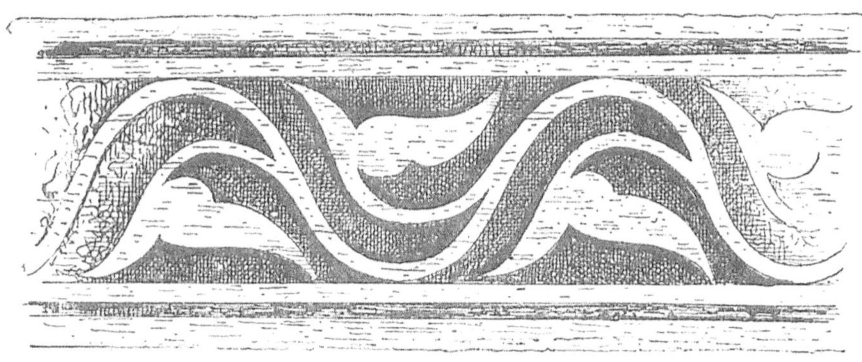

ELEVENTH LESSON.

DIAPER-WORK—STAMPED DIAPER-PATTERNS— CUTTING DIAPERS.

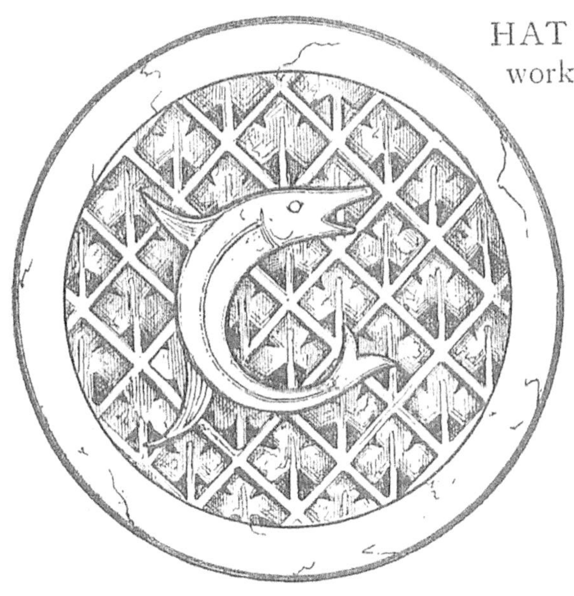

HAT which is called diaper-work is where the ground consists of one generally small pattern frequently repeated at regular intervals. It is so called from the well-known diaper or figured linen cloth, from the Old French *diapré*, meaning the same, from the verb *diapréz*, to diaper, or "diversifie with flourishings" (Cotgrave). The verb, according to Skeat, is from the Old French *diaspre*, later *jasper*, a stone much used for ornamental jewellery. Italian, *diaspro*, a jasper. "*Diaper*, to decorate with a variety of colours, or to embroider on a rich ground" (Anglo-Norman). "There was a rich figured cloth so called" (Strutt, ii. 6), as "also a kind of printed linen" (Halliwell). The latter are still common. It is, however, most probable that the word really comes, as Fairholt asserts, from Ypres, *i.e.*, d'Ypres, which was famous for such work. Some writers apply the term to merely dotting, indenting, or roughening a ground, but it is properly applicable to small figures.

STAMPED DIAPER PATTERNS. These may be produced firstly and most readily by means of wood, stamped or punched, Fig. 23 and 27, and a hammer or mallet. Practise with these first on waste wood. It is not at first easy to repeat them at perfectly regular intervals, making one the same as the other. The work is greatly facilitated by drawing lines like a chequer or chess-board on the ground, and making a stamp or diaper in every dot, or all along the lines. Punches for this purpose may be had in great variety. This class of stamped work is very effective for narrow edgings and borders, and on fillets, which would otherwise be tedious and difficult to carve. With but little practice this work can be executed with great rapidity.

CUTTING DIAPERS. There are some patterns which are very easily cut with a single tool, as, for instance, squares, diamonds, and triangles. For these a firmer or chisel is sufficient. The reader will observe that one square, etc., is removed alternately, and another left. In designing or selecting these, or any diapers, care must be taken to choose such as fit together exactly. But any figures of this kind, whatever they are, are well adapted for grounds.

A more advanced style of diaper-work is made by cutting lines with the parting-tool or smallest gouge, unless, indeed, you are expert enough to do it with a chisel or firmer.

This was the commonest kind of diapering on caskets in the Middle Ages. A very pretty effect was often produced by filling

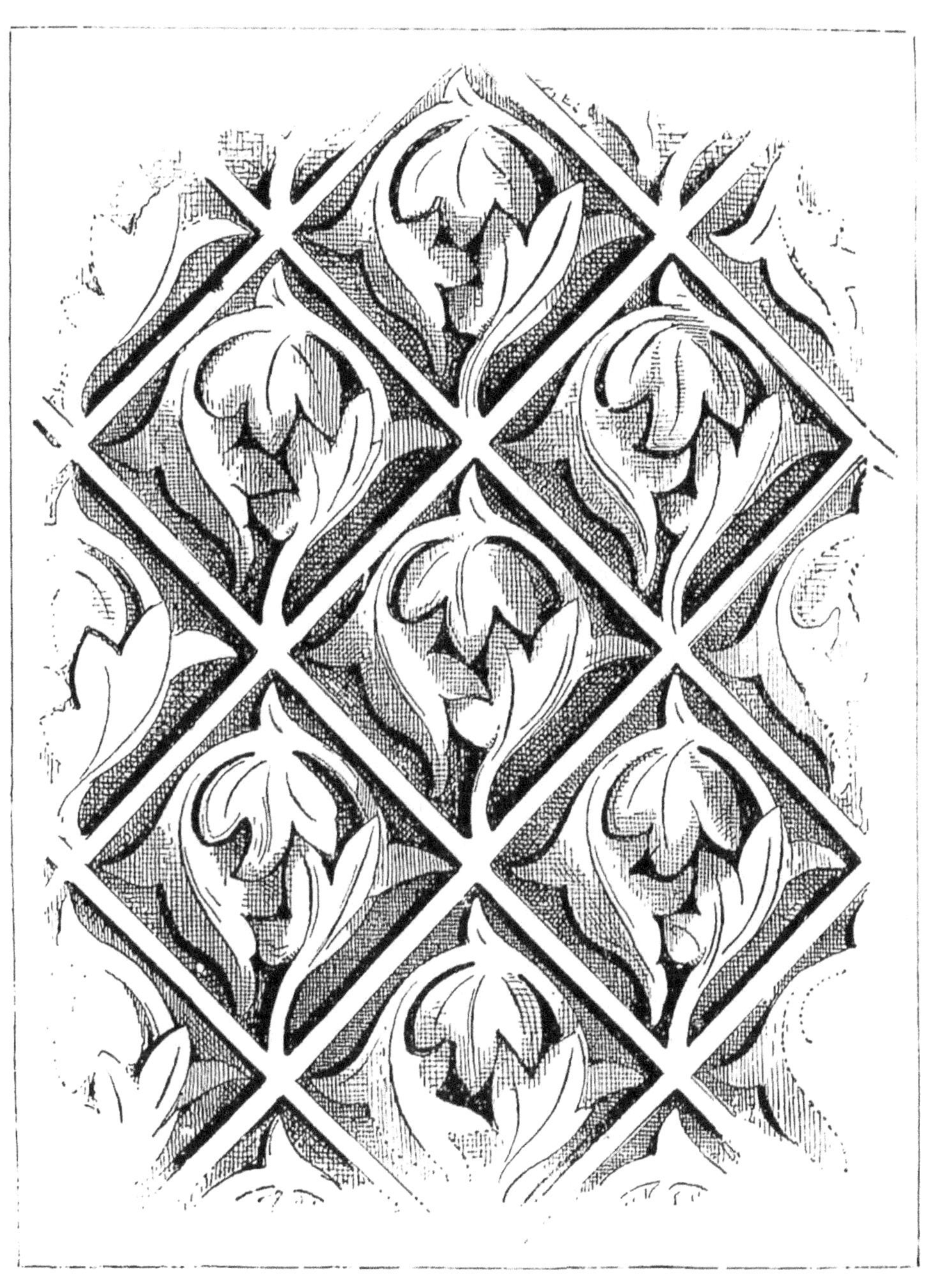

Fig. 50.

A SINGLE DIAPER REPEATED.

these lines with dark brown or black paint. In any case, when oiled, or as they grew old, and dust and oil or moisture worked into them, they became dark. It has already been said that any kind of mere *line*-work can be executed on a smooth wooden surface by means of a V tool, or generally by a small gouge. It may also be effected with a tracing-wheel, or with a tracer, or with any rather dull-pointed instrument. In hard wood of a light colour very beautiful effects may thus be produced.

The next step is to cut lines, and combine with these cutting out and excavating spaces, as in ordinary carving. Nevertheless, it is not, as a rule, a good plan to make diapers too ornamental or elaborate ; for this will lead to making them large, and then they will draw attention from the pattern, if there is one, or the main figures. When the whole surface is all diaper, as in a carpet, the diapers may be as large and as elaborate as one chooses to make them.

There is but one general rule for designing the diaper. Draw a chess-board, and then by diagonals convert these into " points up and down," squares, or triangles ; or fill the equal spaces with equilateral triangles, hexagons, circles, or pentagons, etc.[1] These may be filled in with any suitable decoration. In Fig. 50 portions of the original surface of the panel have been left as ridges to separate the diapers, and then every one of the latter has been carved with the same ornament ; a rather advanced example, but cut only in moderate relief. Another plate, Fig. 52, gives a variety of suitable figures in low relief; some two or three of these should be chosen and repeated in regular order in neighbouring spaces.

Where the main object is simple decoration of surfaces, plain diaper-cutting is an important industry, and one by means of which, with no very great degree of skill, beautiful results may be

[1] To draw these and ornament them, consult " Drawing and Designing," by C. G. Leland ; London, Whittaker and Co.

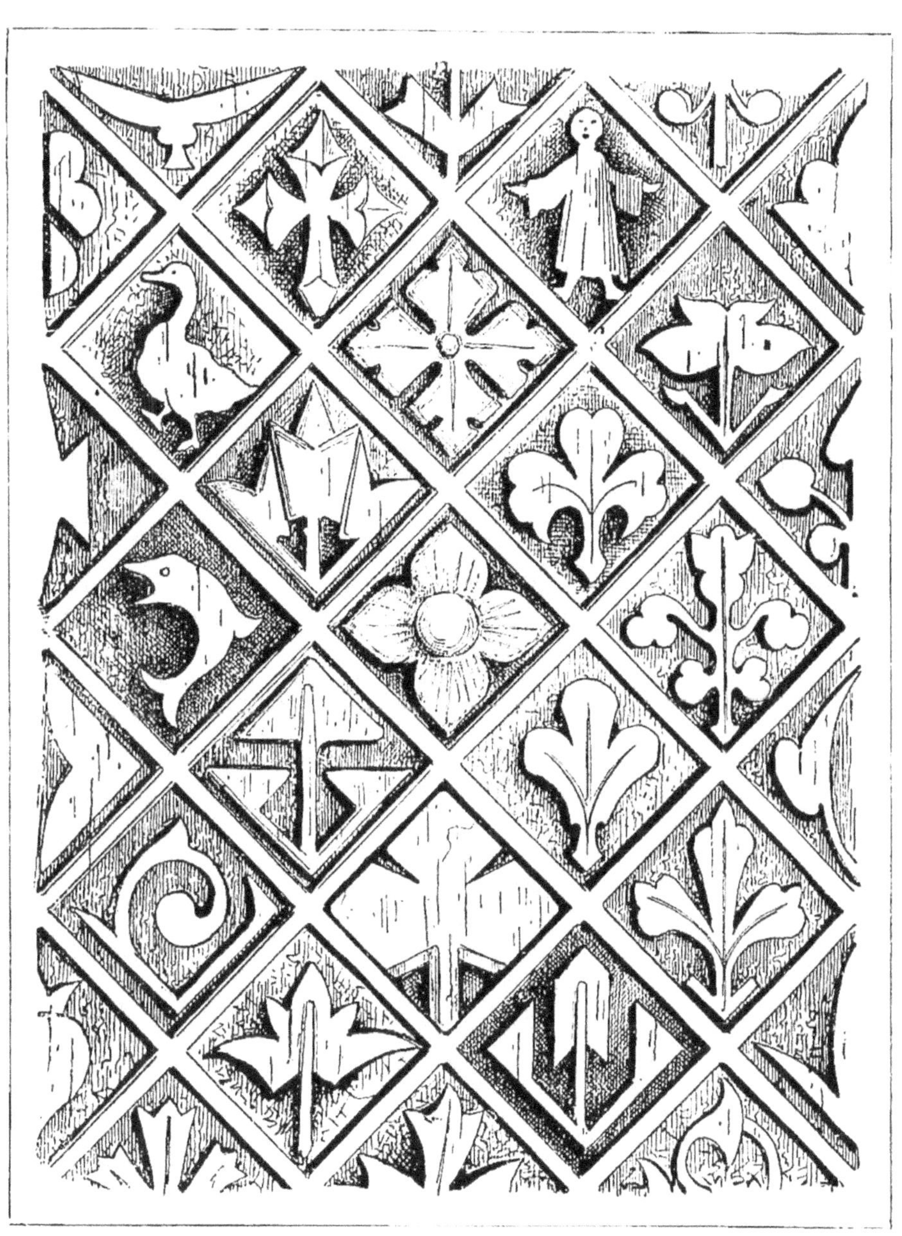

Fig. 51.
A VARIETY OF DIAPER PATTERNS.

obtained.   Thus, large pieces of furniture, chests, and especially walls or wainscoats, may be expeditiously adorned by means of it, even by one who is far from being able to carve in the round or cut leaves.   It may be very much facilitated in many ways, One of these is to cut out the patterns in duplicate, many at once in paper, paste them on the wood, and carve round them. Then wet the paper, and thoroughly remove it with a stiff brush. Another plan is to cut out the pattern in card-board, thin brass, or wood, and stencil it with a lead pencil or colour which will wash off.   Then cut away as before.   It is extremely easy, when we have once cut a certain figure a few times, to go on repeating it, and beginners can, therefore, with great advantage, be set at diaper-cutting, since they thereby acquire not only a familiarity with the use of the tools, but by dint of repetition familiarize themselves perfectly with at least one process; for the greatest trouble in all arts and studies is, that they do not, at any early step, sufficiently master any one thing.

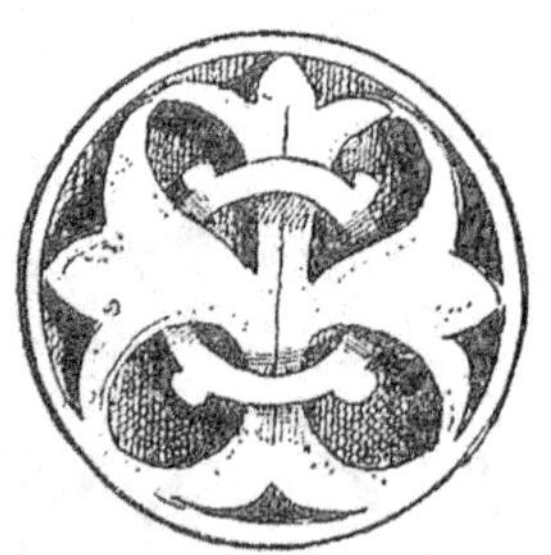

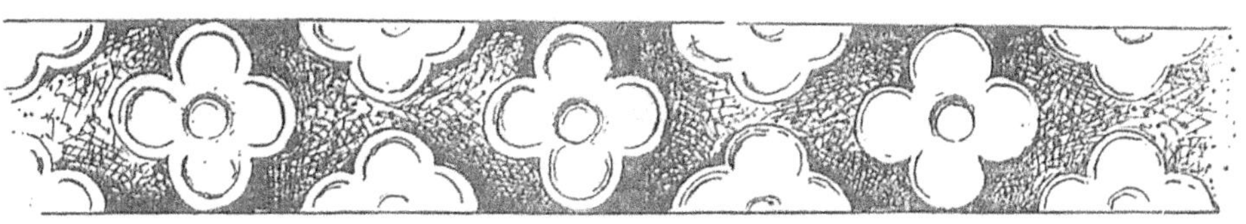

TWELFTH LESSON.

BUILDING-UP, OR APPLIQUÉ WORK.

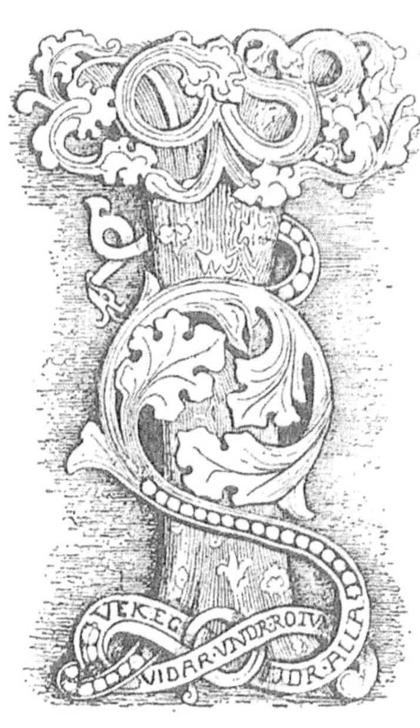

IT will often happen that in carving, while most of the work is on a level, some portion, generally the centre, will rise above the rest, or project beyond it, illustrated by Fig. 12. It would often be a waste of wood and time to cut this out of a single piece. In such cases we merely glue an extra piece of wood on, and carve it into shape. Sometimes in carving a face, only the nose, and perhaps the chin, require to be added. It is said that this method of gluing wood on to wood to obtain additional relief was first extensively practised by Grinling Gibbons.

In Germany this addition of a central "boss" is so well understood, that in many shops they sell heads or faces of men, women, or animals, wreaths, and similar centres or bosses for carvers who can execute flat or ribbon-work, but not high relief. In this way very ornamental or showy pieces of work may be executed with the least possible pains and expense. In the same manner a piece of old carving, or, it may be, several pieces, are taken or saved from some half-ruined ancient specimen, and well glued on a sound piece of old wood exactly like them in colour and texture. This is then carved in the same style. In this way really valuable work may be easily made, for such half-decayed pieces of old carving are too often thrown away, and may often be purchased for a trifle.

Still, this method of *appliqué*, or applied wood on wood, though it may be resorted to in certain cases to save a great deal of cutting and material, may be carried too far, when it degenerates into mere manufacture.

Appliqué work of this kind falls still further into manufacture when it consists of thin boards, cut into patterns with a fret or scroll-saw, worked up with gouges, and then glued on wood. This is plain imitation. Yet it may be borne in mind, though most writers on the subject deny it, that while it is absolutely *not* high or legitimate art, there is no law and no reason against it ; and if a man can contrive no better way to ornament his house, he is perfectly in the right in doing so, if he thinks fit. And it he can afford the time, skill, and materials, he will probably advance from *appliqué* work to something better. In any case he will have learned something by it, and it is worth learning. It is too often the case with high art critics, that they exact that everybody *must* have finished taste and *high* perceptions all at once, with no regard to expense.

The pupil may now attempt an easy piece of *appliqué* work. Take a panel, Fig. 52, and trace on it the pattern. Leave a blank flat space of the original surface, called the " seat," for the figures, of their precise size, and then work out the ground. Where this consists of a *diaper*, it may be made either by carving or by stamping. Having finished the diapered ground,

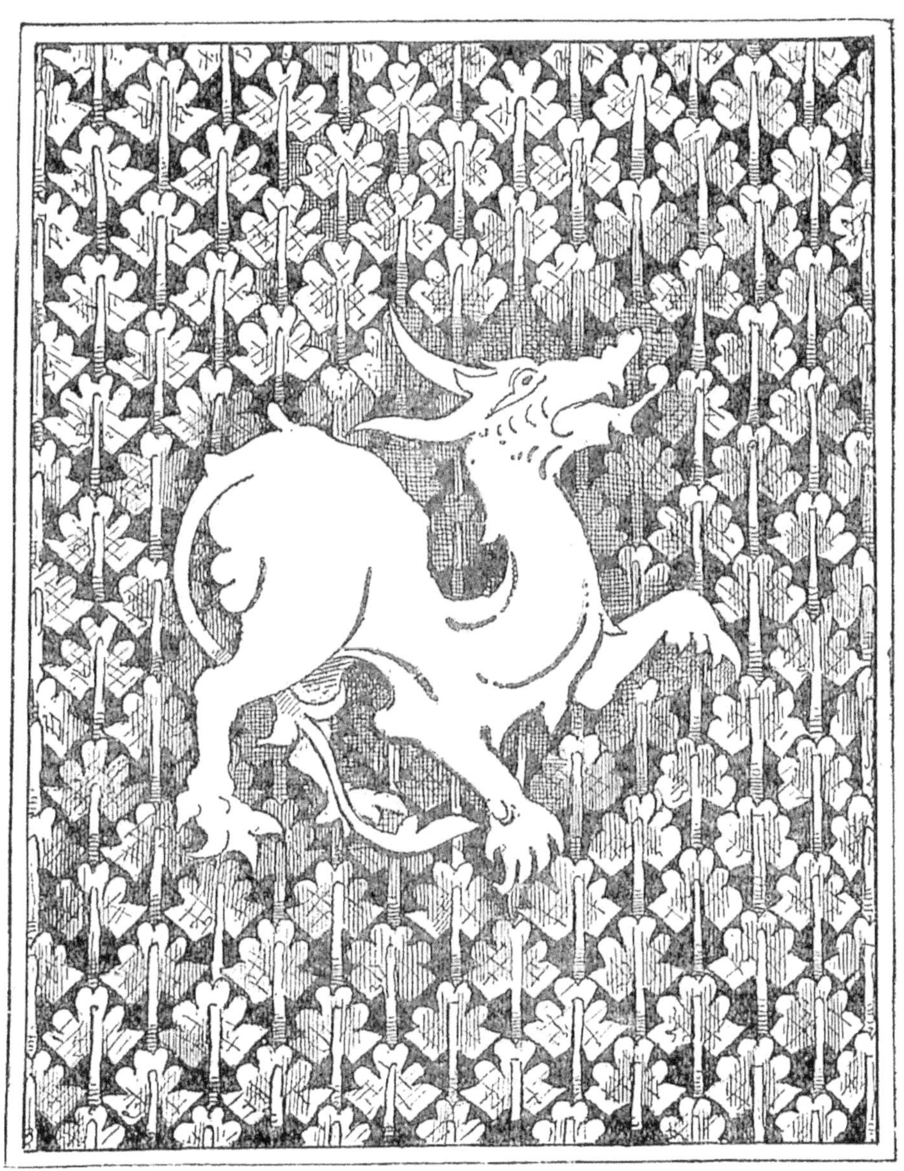

Fig. 52. Appliqué Work.

Dragon in Thin Wood, Appliqué on a Diaper Ground.

saw or cut out the figures, glue them into their places, and carve them ; or the carving may be executed before the application.

Appliqué work is liable to the objection, especially where large surfaces are laid on, that two pieces of wood are seldom of *precisely* the same quality and texture, and that, therefore, they may sometimes afterwards shrink or swell in different directions, with the natural result of warping and splitting. This is sometimes remedied by using screws as well as glue ; but the best preventive of such accidents is to cut both the ground and the piece glued on to it from the same piece of wood, of course perfectly seasoned.

In many cases frames or borders may be *appliqué* or glued on. If the work be intended for an album or book-cover, the frame may be made a trifle higher than the central ornament, to protect it from being scratched when lying with the face on any surface. This will not be necessary if it be used for a panel in the side of a box or in a wall.

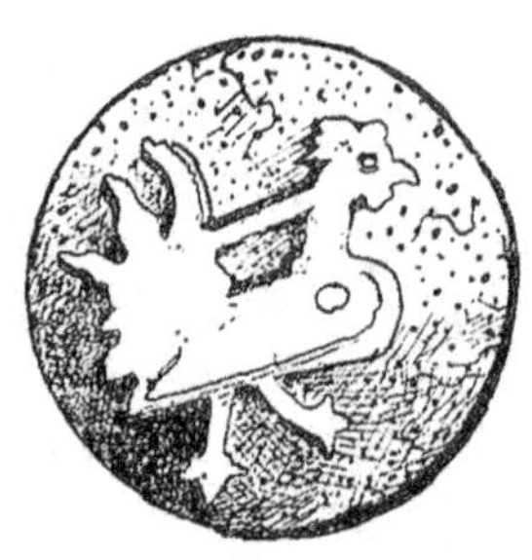

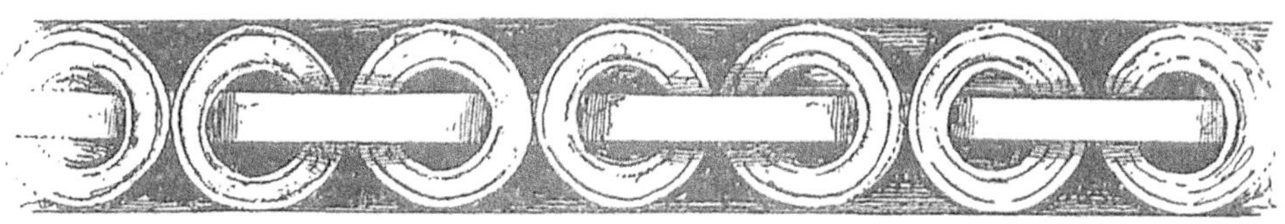

THIRTEENTH LESSON.

CARVING IN THE ROUND.

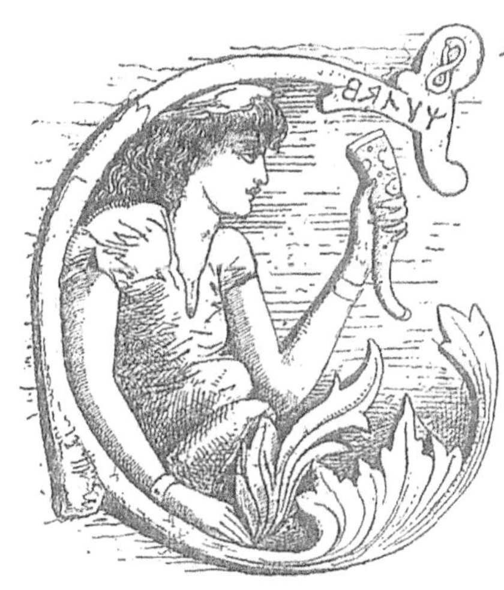

ARVING in the round is cutting an object which is finished on every side, as a bust or statue. It is in fact "statuary." It seems to be very difficult work to a beginner, but the pupil who has mastered the rudiments which are laid down in this book, and who can measure and cut a low relief of an inch, or a high relief pattern of two or three inches, will find no trouble whatever in carving something small in the round, and in progressing from this to something larger. The steps in wood-carving from hammering an indented pattern to carving a statue are perfectly defined, and very easy if they are thoroughly mastered one at a time.

Carving in the round will be least difficult to the one who can model his work in clay or modelling-wax. This is especially easy if he alternates carving with designing and modelling ; it is, in fact, so great an aid to carving, that there should be little of the latter without it. He who has modelled anything in clay or wax has, in a way, carved it in a soft material, while true carving is only modelling with gouges and chisels.

There is no difficulty for one who has mastered the first six lessons of this book, in carving half a duck or fish in relief. If he could carve the other side and join them he would have the animal complete. From blocking out simple forms, such as ducks, fish, hares, or game, in high relief, the carver soon learns how to "rough" almost anything. Having made a bust in clay, he knows where a bit is to be removed or cut away here or there. He studies it as he proceeds, alternately in profile or full-face, and continually measures with callipers and compasses to see that he is preserving all the proportions. The practice which he has had in delicately carving, grooving, sweeping, and modelling leaves, in cutting the hair of game, imitating basket-work, etc., will all now come into play. As regards fitting certain tools to form the eye-balls, eye-lids, etc., if the pupil does not as yet know the measure and capacity of his tools, he has worked to little purpose. If he should be in doubt from time to time, let him just carve an eye, or a lip, or mouth, on a piece of waste wood, and he will have no difficulty in repeating it; and he who grudges the time for such practice will never make an artist, Fig. 53.

The great difficulty in carving in deep relief and in the round, is to get the general sweep and .contour and proportions of the *whole*, and this is difficult for a pupil who does not design, and shade, and model, while it is a mere trifle to one who does. The cutting and blocking out, which seems to be the great difficulty, is a merely mechanical process, performed with compasses, carving tools, and rasps, and sometimes with a steel bow-saw, here and there. And it presents no difficulties to any intelligent person who has carefully executed all that is described in the previous lessons, especially to one who has carved animals and simple figures, or faces, in high relief.

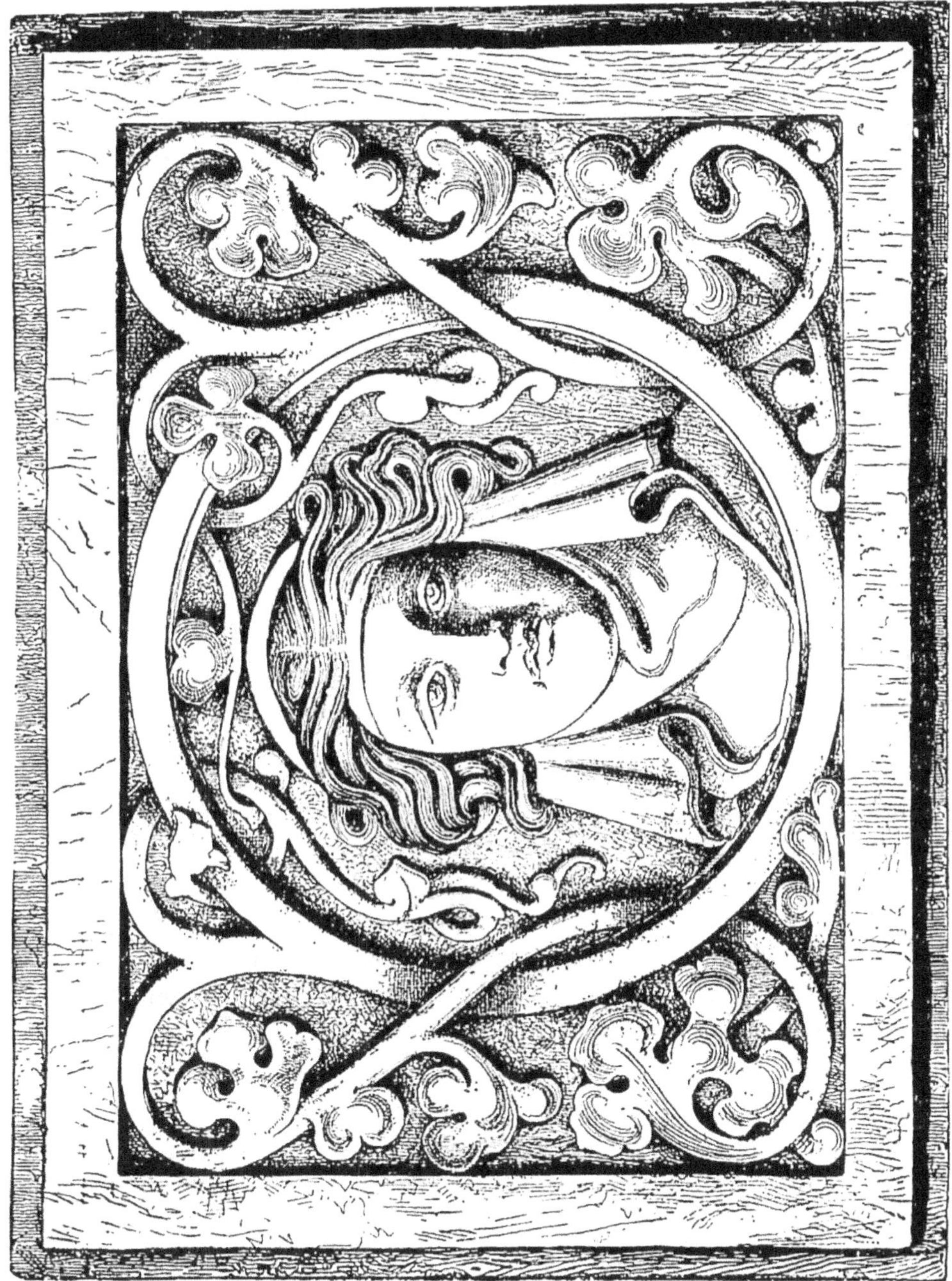

Fig. 53.   HIGH RELIEF.   Design by C. G. Leland.

It is true that in shops where much large and coarse work is executed, as, for instance, great pieces for ceilings, figures for façades, and the like, the sculptor, trained from the beginning to the sweep-cut and to bold chipping, makes little account of any difficulty, and proceeds to carve with great confidence. Now what the student must endeavour to attain is some of the confidence of the mere workman with the culture and knowledge of the artist. And he should, whenever an opportunity presents itself, try to see practical carvers of all kinds at work, for in this way he will learn much which no books give.

It is to be recommended that the first attempts at carving in the round be made in soft pine wood, as it is of course most easily modelled. No one should be discouraged because a first or second effort has turned out a failure.

I have observed that many writers on the art treat carving in high relief, or in the round, as if the first effect in it must necessarily be a human head or figure, that is to say, the most difficult of all objects. But he who can cut out a wooden shoe, or a rabbit, or a fish, or the simplest object, on a large scale, on all its sides, will, if he repeats this till he can do it easily, have mastered the greatest difficulty which alarms beginners, that of *blocking out* from all sides.

In the head by Civitale, full half-round, which may easily be made full round, the carver may begin by modelling the whole. If this is not convenient, let him mark out with the compasses the different dimensions, and carefully bring the whole into form by first rounding all into a rude shape, and then very gradually cut away the hollows. No detailed descriptions of exactly what tools to choose for certain places, or how to work, would be of any real use to the pupil who has carefully executed the previous lessons, as he will not have a single cut which he has not made before, and in this instance a little voluntary ingenuity and reflection will do more good than any instruction.

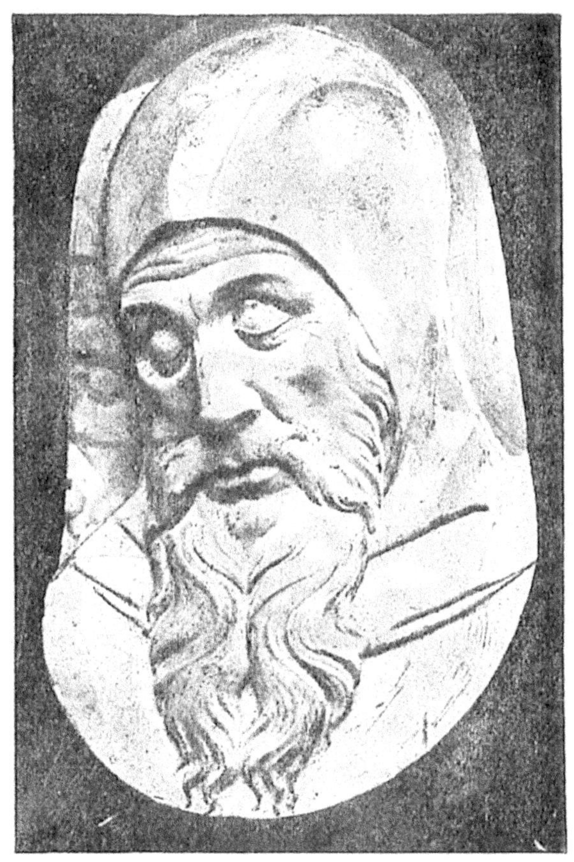

HEAD, BY CIVITALE.   *P.* 82.

APPENDIX TO LESSON XIII.

ON THE USE OF THE SAW.

(*By John J. Holtzapffel.*)

THE steel buhl saw-frame (Fig. 16) may be very usefully employed for removing many of the superfluous portions of the material in the earliest stages of carving in the round, as in large or small figurini, and for those parts which have to be cut away to leave the outlines or margins between leaves and other ornaments in flat works. In such cases it is to be recommended, for its use not only saves much time, but also the risk of breakages, to which the work is very liable when these portions have to be removed entirely with the carving-tool.

In round carving, the block, more or less roughly marked out on its surfaces to some approach to its ultimate form with thick pencil or crayon lines, may be held on the work-bench by the carver's screw (Fig. 10), or if that be not convenient, or if it be flat work, it can be held in the vice. A coarse strong buhl saw-blade is employed; this is first fixed in the screw jaw at the further side of the saw-frame; the handle of the latter is then unscrewed until it projects its jaw about half-an-inch, and at the moment the other end of the blade is fixed therein, the two jaws are also made to approach one another by pressing the further side of the saw-frame against the work-bench, with the handle against the workman's chest; after this, the handle is screwed back again until its jaw returns home to its former position. The back of the saw-blade is towards the back of the saw-frame, and the teeth of the blade should point away from the handle, easily discovered by passing the finger along them, and when the saw is properly strained for use it should ring like a harp string.

In use, the handle of the frame is grasped by all the fingers of the hand, except the forefinger, which is stretched straight out along it in the direction of the saw ; the latter is pushed straight forward and withdrawn with moderate pressure, just sufficient to cause it to cut, and is twisted about to follow the directions of the lines or curves of the piece to be removed. During the sawing the outstretched forefinger is an unerring guide for the direction of the cut.

When a piece has to be removed from between others which have to be left, as between the body and the bend of the arm, or between the legs of a figure, a small hole is first drilled through the block and the saw threaded through it before it is strained ; and the only necessary precaution throughout in using the saw, is to leave sufficient material everywhere for perfect freedom in the subsequent carving by not cutting anywhere too close.

An entirely different method is followed in cutting out moulds, the pieces to be used for *appliqué* carving, and for the outlines of fretwork or panels pierced with many interstices of which the surface is afterwards to be carved. These works cannot be held fast in the vice or otherwise, not only because they are often thin and liable to fracture, but because, if so held, it is impossible to attain the desired true, easy-flowing outlines required at once without subsequent correction, which can be produced without difficulty when the workis perfectly free.

The professional hand fret-cutter, who produces the best and most elaborate work, such objects as the long, thin, pierced panels to be backed with silk for the fronts of pianofortes, uses a similar, but much deeper, yet light saw-frame made of wood, with the same steel screw-jaws, hung to the ceiling by a cord. He sits astride a bench called " a horse," which has two tall vertical jaws in front of him, their upper edges lined with brass, or sometimes with cork. The further jaw is fixed to withstand the thrust of the saw, the other is notched below and springs open when left to itself, but is closed by a diagonal strut resting loosely in mortise smade in the face of the bench and in that of the movable jaw ; the strut is pulled downwards to close the jaw on the work by means of a cord passing from it through a hole in the benιch to a treadle beneath the workman's foot. The surfaces of his work are, therefore, vertical, and the work itself is very lightly held, so that he can twist it about in all directions with the left hand, while he keeps the saw steadily traversing backwards and forwards in the same plane horizontally, with the right.

A simpler support, called a " saw table," Fig. 7 *b*, is used, and thoroughly answers every purpose for the smaller class of works which we are considering. This tool consists of an oblong piece of wood, perfectly flat, smooth and polished on its upper surface, at the one end of which there is a slot of about an inch wide ; beneath, it has a cross piece of wood to keep the implement steady on the bench or table on which it is placed, and a clamp and screw to fix it there.

The work, first pierced with the holes for threading the saw through all its intended interstices, has the saw placed through one of them, strained as before, and is then laid down, pattern uppermost, on the saw table, upon which it is lightly held and twisted about by the points of all five fingers of the left hand planted vertically upon it; the saw is worked up and down vertically in the slot by the right hand, the handle below the saw table. The aim here is to keep the saw working always in the same place, and to let the curve or line result from the perfectly free movement of the work alone. The saw-blades employed are much finer than those previously referred to ; they are tightly strained in the same way as before, but they are placed in the frame so that the teeth now point the reverse way, towards the handle, and the cut, therefore, takes place at the downward stroke.

The saws in ordinary use, such as the brass-backed tenon and dove-tail saws and the key-hole saws of the carpenter, also find constant employment in first roughly shaping and preparing the blocks and panels to be subsequently carved ; in their use it is only necessary, as in all sawing upon carved works, to cut just sufficiently wide of the lines marked to ensure that all saw-marks will be removed by the carving tool.

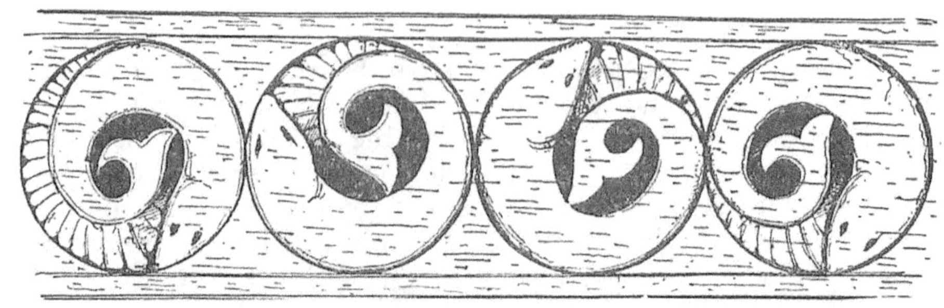

FOURTEENTH LESSON.

INCISED, INTAGLIO, OR SUNK CARVING.

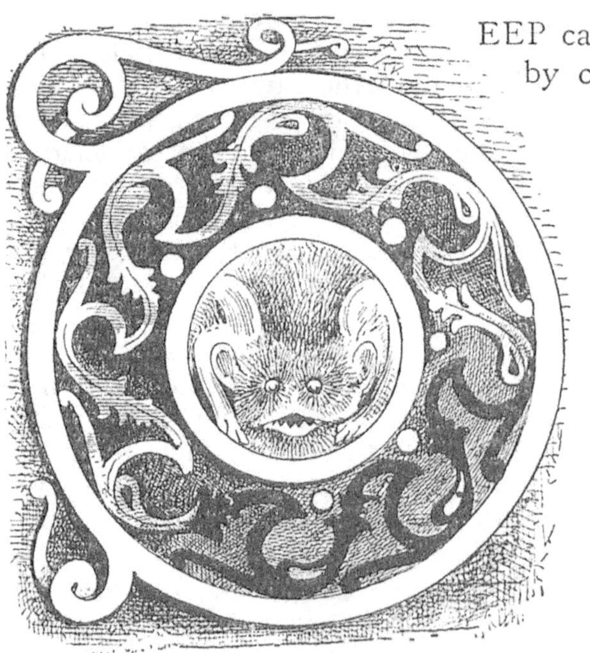

EEP carving, as it is termed by certain writers, is now known among artists as incised, sunk, or intaglio. It is an advanced form of gouge-cutting.

It is a very beautiful yet easy kind of work, which was extensively practised in Italy in early times, and which is deserving special attention because of its applicability not only to bold, large, and even coarse decoration—which was, however, very effective—but to the most delicate and minute objects. "It may," says General

Fig. 54.   Incised Carving.

Seaton, who was the first to describe it, which he does with much enthusiasm, " be called sunk carving, for, contrary to the usual method, the carving is sunk, while the ground is left at its original level."   Like engraving on metal, it cuts into the ground, and depends entirely on outline, or drawing, and shadow for its effects.   It is suitable for book-covers, or to be employed wherever the carving is liable to be handled or rubbed, because, being sunk beneath the ground, it cannot be rubbed or injured till the ground itself is worn down.

Take any wood except a coarse one,—holly, beech, oak, poplar, pear, or walnut,—and let the surface be well planed, or perhaps polished.   If it be a wood of light colour, draw your pattern with a very soft pencil, say *B B B*, on paper, lay it face down on the wood, and rub the back carefully with an ivory or other polisher.   The work is chiefly executed with bent gouges and grainers, flat and hollow, with two or three bent chisels and stamps, and it often happens that a good piece of incised carving can be executed with very few tools.   It is executed almost entirely by hand, or without hammering.

Choose some simple pattern, your object being to learn how to cut and not to produce something startling at a first effort. If the wood be dark, such as American walnut, mark the pattern through with the prick-wheel or dot, Fig. 54.   If the pupil has not perfect eyesight, or expects to carve at night, it is advisable to outline this dot line with a very fine camel's hair brush and Chinese white.   This prevents many mistakes.   Take, to begin, a small gouge, a little less than the stem to be cut in diameter, and run it along the line.   When you cut leaves, get gradually towards the centre.   Then take a larger gouge and finish the stems.

Keep by you a piece of clay or putty, or moist kneaded bread, and from time to time take an impression of your work. This is important, for the real excellence of intaglio carving

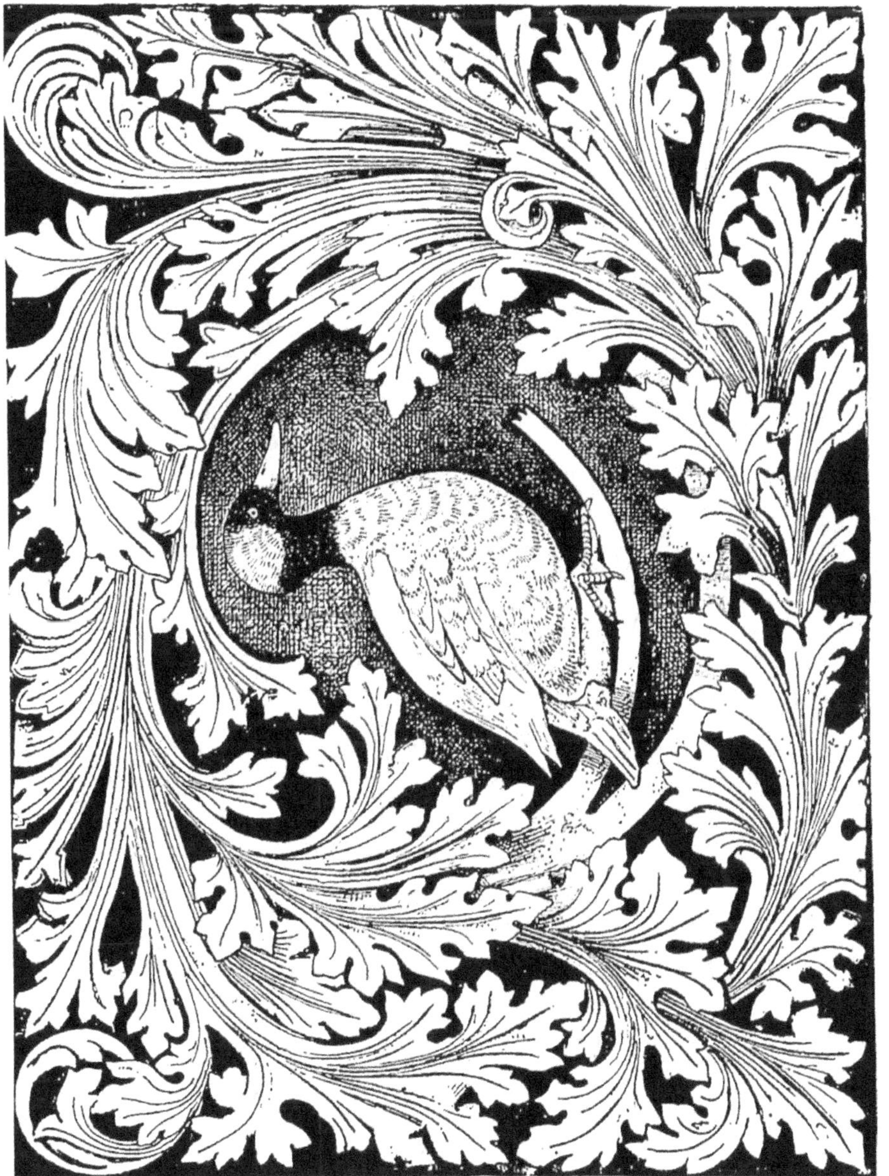

Fig. 55. Incised Border. Centre in Low Relief.

consists in its being exactly like relief carving reversed. In this way you will at once perceive, without any special directions, what tools to use in your work.

Fig. 55 is a rather advanced example of this class of carving. The whole of the foliage is cut in cavo relievo, or cavities, with gouges and chisels, both straight and bent, and the lines upon them with bent V tools. The duck in the centre may be in ordinary low relief, to give an effective contrast.

There is another reason for thus learning to make your work perfect. If you carve in hard wood, you can always use a piece of sunk or intaglio carving for a mould. When it is finished take a piece of russet leather, soak it in water till it is quite soft, press it with your fingers and a sponge for some time with great care into the mould, and then take it off. If your wood be well cut, the leather when dry will be quite as attractive as the carving itself, and may be used in many ways. The wood will not be injured in the least if you wipe it dry after taking the impression. With such moulds *papier-maché* casts can also be taken. I have now before me a beautiful specimen of old Byzantine work made in this manner.

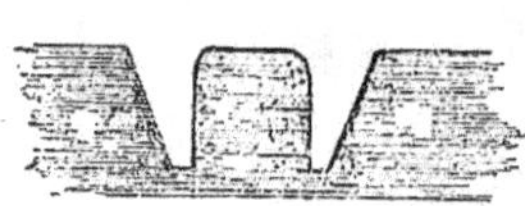

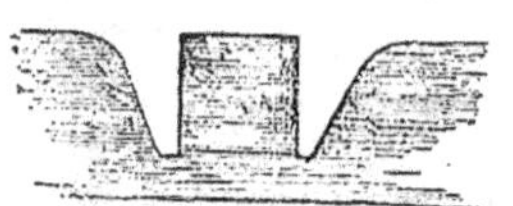

Egpytian Cutting.

There is a peculiar kind of intaglio carving which may be called Egyptian, because the ancient Egyptians used it very extensively on their monuments. It consisted of cutting out the outline of a figure in the following manner. On the *outside* the carver cut down perpendicularly, while the inside pattern was not cut away, but only had its edges rounded.

The result of this peculiar groove or cut, straight on one side and rounded or curved on the other, was a very strong relief and shadow. It was in fact a simple combination of relief and incised or cavo carving, by means of which a strong relief was attained by little work. The main object was to make the inscription solid and durable, and at the same time very legible. The principle, as I have shown, is quite applicable to ornament, and requires much less labour than even intaglio carving. It is something more, in fact much more, than mere outlining, and it is particularly applicable to mural or wall decoration.

Incised carving is often much improved by being painted, and sometimes varnished. That is to say, the sunken portion is thus coloured. I have seen white and vermilion used with good effect, but black and dark brown are generally preferred. Gilding seems peculiarly rich when thus applied in the hollow, as the shadow gives it a fine tone.

Though the imitation of engravings is not within the range of wood-carving, there is, however, a very pretty and easy art by which drawing and painting are very ingeniously combined with a kind of carving. Take a panel of firm wood of lightish colour, well planed and polished. Draw on it any pattern, or even an animal, or human figures. Incise the principal lines with a V tool, or, according to its size, small gouges may be used. For the fine lines and shading, a tracer, or any point to indent, not so sharp as to scratch; this is a matter of great importance; and the wood, which, if possible, should be of box, sycamore, beech, or holly, must be adapted or prepared to take a mark without breaking. When all the lines are well in, take a miniature fitch pencil, and fill in every line with colour, taking care not to let the paint spread beyond the lines. Different colours may be used. This is hardly wood-carving at all, but in skilful hands it produces beautiful and remarkable effects. It is very effective indeed when applied to leather. As the colour is *sunk* in the lines, it is well protected; this kind of ornamentation is therefore well adapted to book-covers. I have applied it successfully to heavy card-board panels prepared for artists to paint on in oil.

As I have said, incised cutting will be found useful to workers in leather, papier-maché, clay, or plaster of Paris, because by means of it they can make moulds. Another kind of mould is made as follows : Cut out with a saw the outline of the pattern in a piece of board thick enough to give the requisite depth. Then glue the perforated board to another board, the surfaces of both being of course first planed and smoothed. This gives the mould in the rough. Then fill in the angles of the hollows with a composition of clay and size, or putty, or rice and lime with white of egg, or any other suitable cement, and while it is soft shape it with fingers and tools to the details of the pattern required. When perfectly dry go over it carefully, taking proofs here and there with putty, and correct with bent files. Then smooth it where it is at all rough, oil it all, and make your cast.

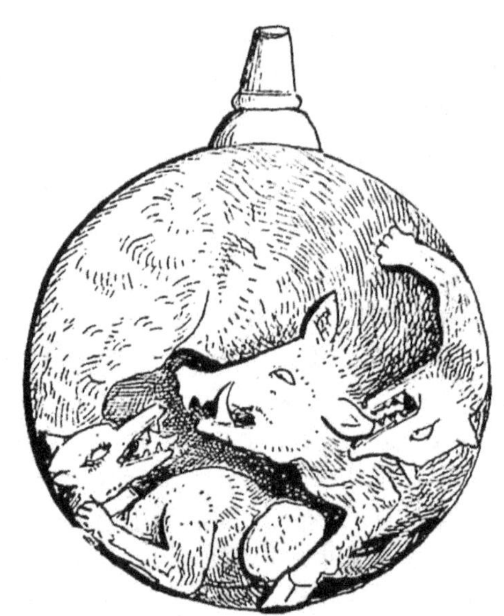

BOXWOOD POWDER FLASK. OLD GERMAN.

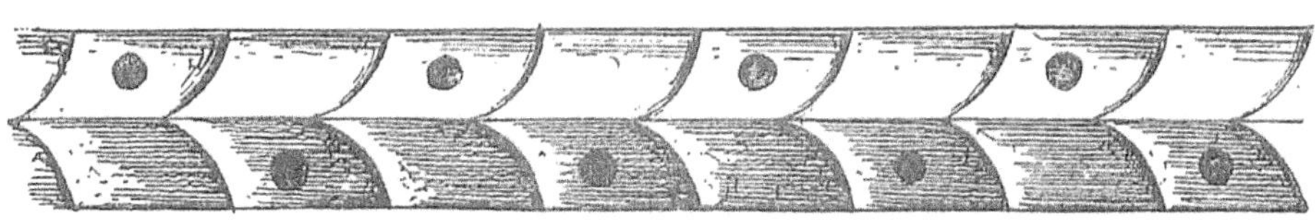

FIFTEENTH LESSON.

CARVING CURVED SURFACES : COCOA-NUTS, BOWLS, HORNS, CASKS, TANKARDS, ETC.

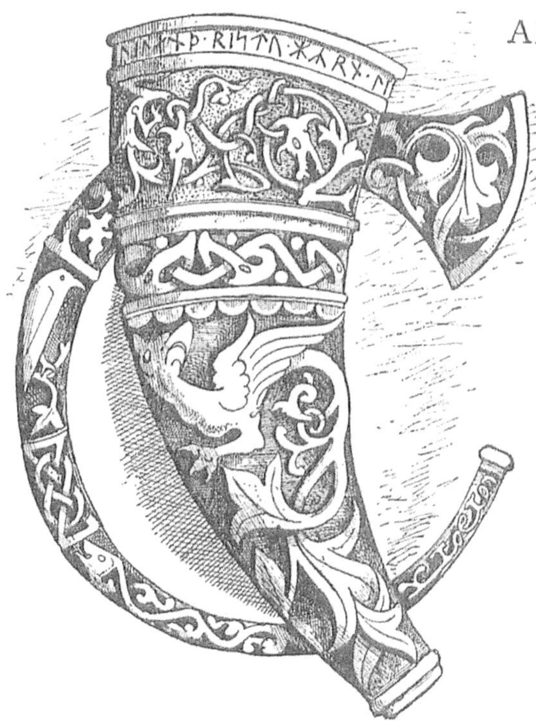

ARVING concave or convex surfaces, such as the exterior of a horn or the interior of a bowl, is often very difficult work, and though an ingenious artist will readily find out for himself some way to get over such difficulties, it is well to know at once how the work may be done.

HORNS. The first difficulty is to fix the object so as to cut it. A beginner who undertakes to carve such a very hard, slippery, and unmanageable object as a horn, will, if he hold it with one hand while he carves with

the other, inevitably damage his pattern or wound himself.
It is very dangerous to hold the work in one hand or
between the knees. One way to secure such an object is to
take a board, nail cross-pieces on it over the ends of the horn
so that a portion may be exposed on which to work, and in
this manner one can cut with safety. Again, holdfasts and
clamps may be employed, but the utmost care should be taken
lest these slip away whenever too great pressure is brought
to bear on them. A very good means to keep the horn firm is
to have a piece of wood fast to the table in which there is a hole,
into which the lesser end of the horn fits, while the butt rests,
and is fixed, on the table. Having secured it, outline the pattern
with a V tool or very small graining-gouge, and then cut away
the ground with quarter-flat, and finally with flat gouges. The
bent file may be freely used for a horn, and it will be necessary
in many places. When bosted, finish with careful touching or
fine files and glass-paper.

If you wish to colour the horn, select one which is chiefly
white. Take a solution of nitrate of silver, which any chemist
will prepare for you. Be very careful indeed how you handle
it, for it will burn clothes, carpets, or flesh, and at least stain
your fingers for a long time. With a *glass brush,* if you can get
one, if not, with a glass point, or pen, or agate point, or wax,
apply the acid carefully to the pattern. If you use wood for this
purpose it will answer, but it is very speedily consumed by the
acid. This will make a yellow, or brown, or sometimes a black
stain, according to the strength of the solution, the number of
times it is applied, and the hardness of the horn. When the
horn is covered with diaper-work, or a great many small figures,
or a close pattern, then always put the acid into the hollows,
and leave the design in white. A black dye for horn, as well
as for metal, is made by combining ammonia with sulphur. It
is very malodorous, but is effective. Any chemist will make

it, and will also prepare for you the dyes used for ivory and horn. It is better and cheaper for the amateur to buy these than to attempt to make them for himself. In most cases black and brown are the best colours to use.

If a horn is boiled in hot water, or steamed, it will become so soft that it may be flattened. Then it is very easy to carve. The author has in his possession two very ancient and singularly ornamented Italian horns which were thus shaped. Horn, when treated with quick-lime and hot water, can be reduced to a paste which can be made into any shape like a cement or plaster. It becomes hard again in cold water. All old horns were not used for gunpowder ; many of them were for wine or other liquors ; others were used for blowing ; they all make effective ornaments. Carved horns are handsome ornaments when hung up with cord and tassels. I have made them very attractive by gilding the raised patterns on them.

TO CARVE A BOWL. The exterior of a bowl presents no special difficulty, if it be well clamped down. It may be secured with blocks and nails, or screws. But the *interior* is harder to get at and much harder to cut. This is, of course, chiefly done with bent gouges and chisels. It requires care and patience in cases of special trouble. I have, however, easily succeeded in wearing or wasting away the ground by the process which will be described in carving cocoa-nuts. Wooden bowls, which are well adapted to carving, may be bought cheaply at household furnishing shops. They are of the kind used in every kitchen. They may be mounted on bases, such as any turner can make, to which the bowl should be fastened with a screw and glue. Bowls may be coloured or gilded like horns. They are very useful for many purposes, chiefly to contain visitors' cards or other small objects on the writing, work, or toilet table.

COCOA-NUTS. If it is to be used as a cup, begin by sawing away the end on which is the " monkey face," or so much as is desirable. Sometimes the whole nut is left, to be hung up as an amulet, ornament, or charm, as ostrich eggs are hung up in the East. Then clean it smooth with a large rasp till fit to carve. Draw the pattern on this with Chinese white, that there may be no mistakes. Then fix the nut to the board or table, as with the bowl (*vide* p. 100).

The ground may, with patience, be cut away with flat gouges, and, with practice, this becomes really easy, and more expeditious than one would at first suppose. Or it may be done chiefly with files. But the most rapid manner of working is by a "cut" which is described as follows by Gen. Seaton, who, however, limits it to mere decoration for a ground.

"There is a species of ornament most useful for the bend of branches, and which is to be seen in Swiss carved brackets. This may be called the *zigzag* pattern or ornament. It is intended to represent the cross-fissures and marks that are seen in the bark of some trees at the end of the branches. It is done with a flat or quarter-round gouge, the hand swaying from side to side, and at the same time advancing by alternate steps each corner of the tool."

That is to say, put the tool straight up and down, and *rock* it from side to side, and it will require little practice to learn it. But to use it, not for ornament, but a cut, or rather dig, a *firmer* or chisel is better than a gouge ; nor need we be very particular as to the appearance of the marks made, as they are all, in the end, to be cut or smoothed out. Rock up and down with the firmer, pressing a little flatter than if the object were to only make lines, or so as to scrape away some of the ground. Then from another direction go over this ground, digging and scraping away again. In this manner a shell may be bosted rapidly, and by it one can work at the bottom of a bowl when even the bent tools are of little or no use. When the whole ground is excavated by this process it may be easily smoothed with files or carving tools. The cuttings from cocoa-nut shell, or waste bits, may be kept, and when pounded to a fine powder, and mixed with glue, they make an admirable cement for repairing walnut or other dark wood work.

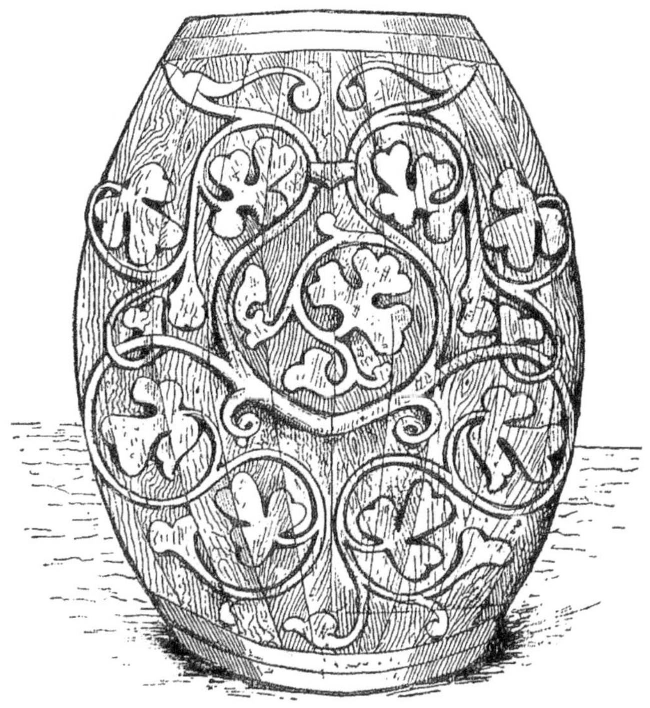

Fig. 56.

CASKS. A cask when carved is an admirable object for waste-papers, or holding canes and umbrellas, Fig. 56. It should be of wood at least one inch in thickness. If held together by broad brass or copper hoops it will be much handsomer. A bucket or pail may be carved in like manner; and when lions' heads or other carved ornaments are *applied*, it will be found that a very ornamental object may be made with little trouble or expense.

It is easiest to carve casks, kegs, buckets, or firkins, up and down,
or in a perpendicular position, and to stand up while at the work,
as a true carver is sure in the end to do at all his work.

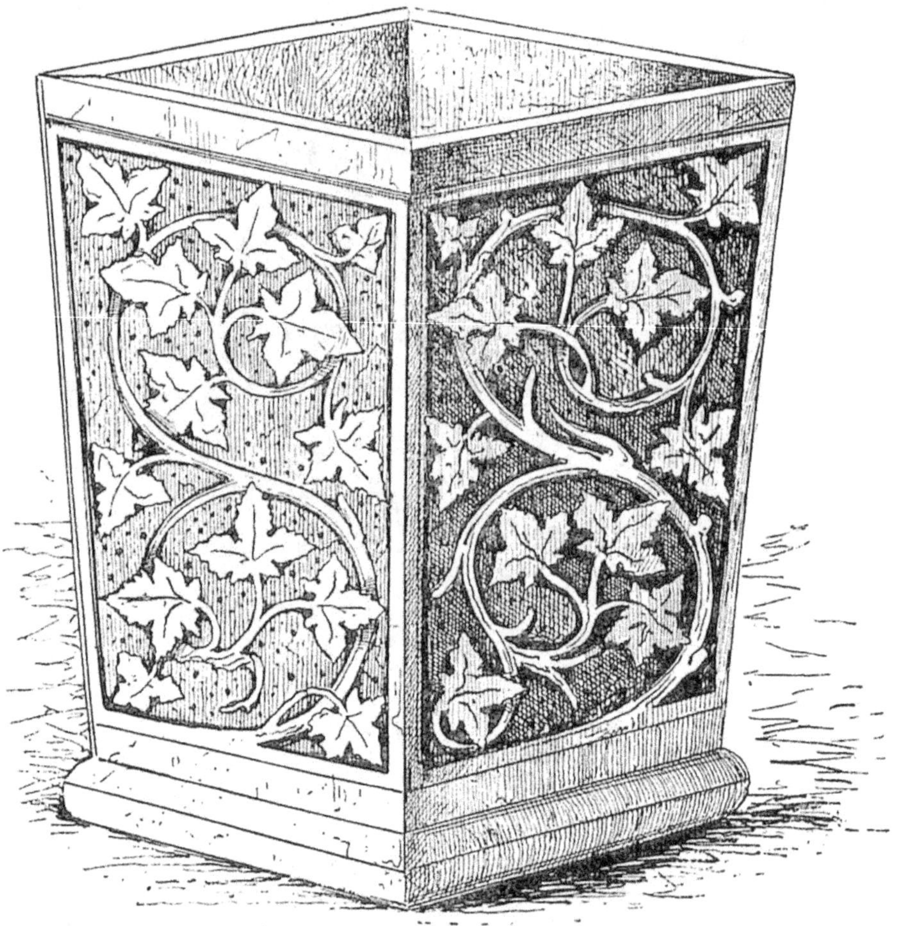

Fig. 57.

TANKARDS AND WASTE-PAPER BOXES. Tankards, if small,
may be turned from solid wood, but, when large, it is best to
have them made by the cooper, of several pieces, and hooped

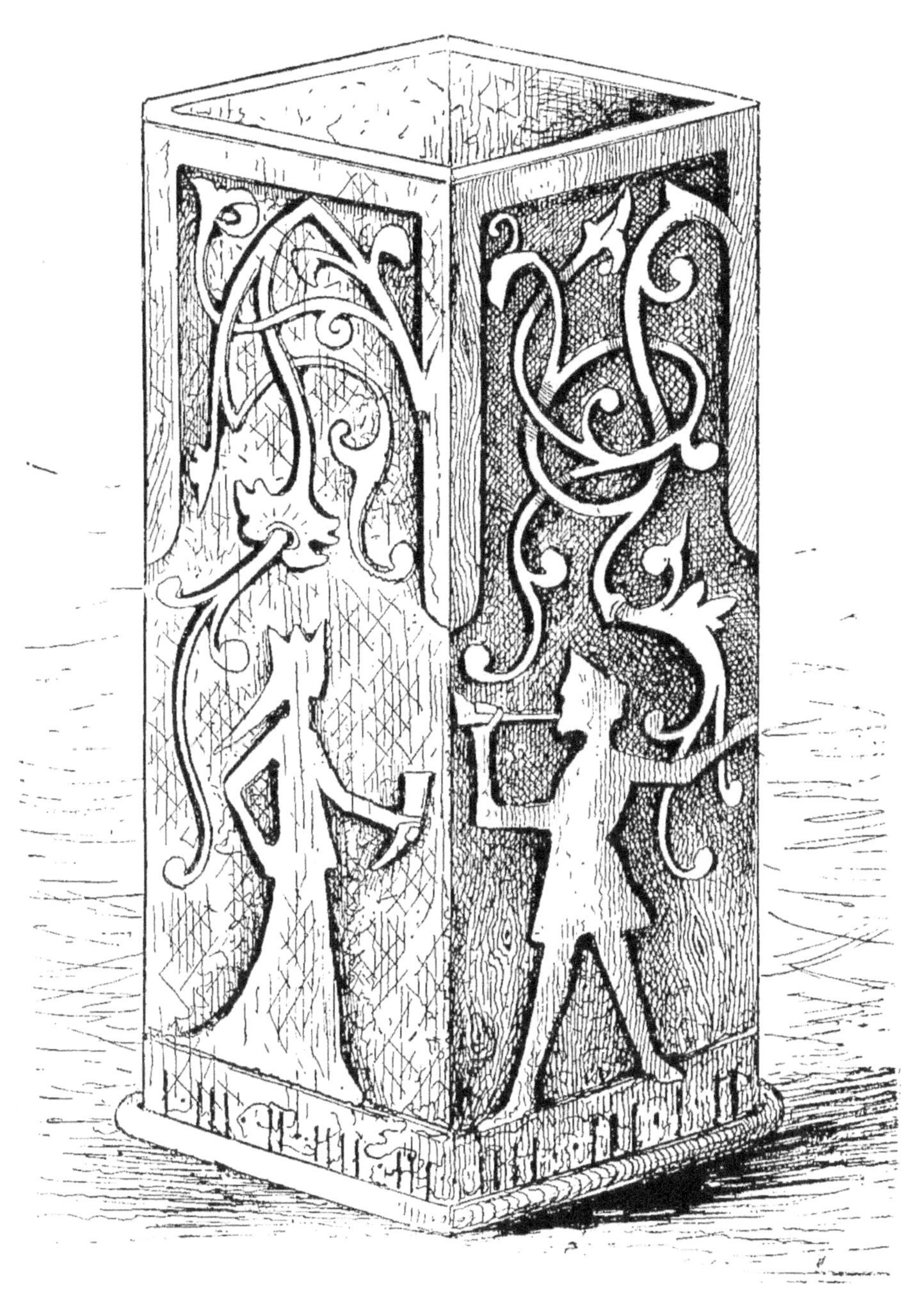

Fig. 58.

OLD IRISH TANKARD.

with metal. To make the design for all such cylindrical objects, take a piece of paper which will *exactly* go round, or correspond to the surface, and be sure to make the pattern continuous, that is, without breaks, unless it be designed in divisions. Wooden measures, such as are used by dealers in nuts, fruit, etc., are well adapted to carving for tankards. They may be bought at general furnishing shops.

The old Irish, and sometimes the Danes, made a rude kind of tankard, Fig. 58, by fastening together with nails, glue, or screws, four pieces of oak panel or thin board. It was like drinking from a box. It makes a useful receptacle for many purposes.

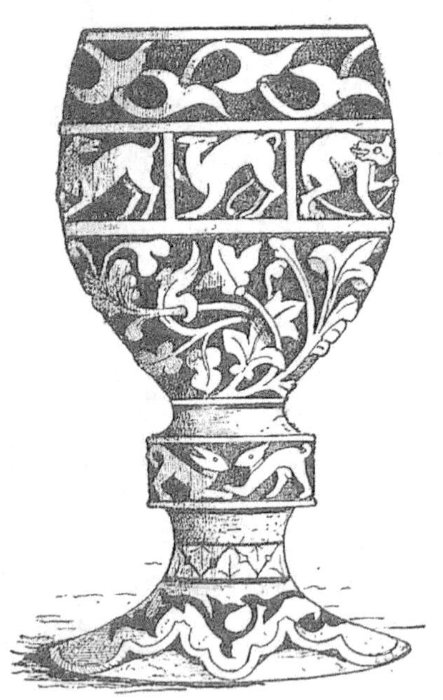

Cocoa-nut Goblet.

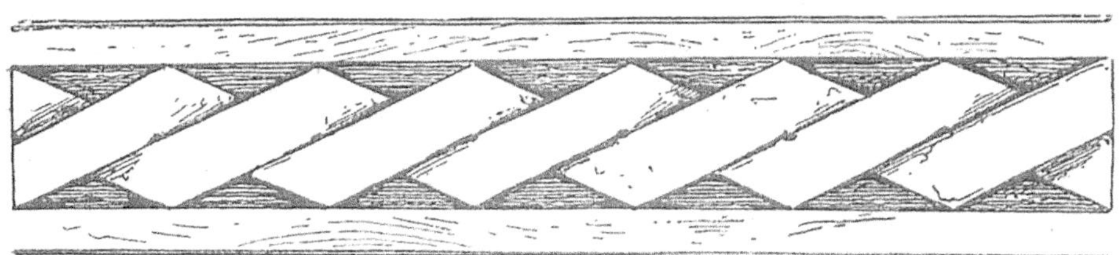

SIXTEENTH LESSON.

BOSSES, KNOBS, BARS, AND POLISHED ORNAMENTS.

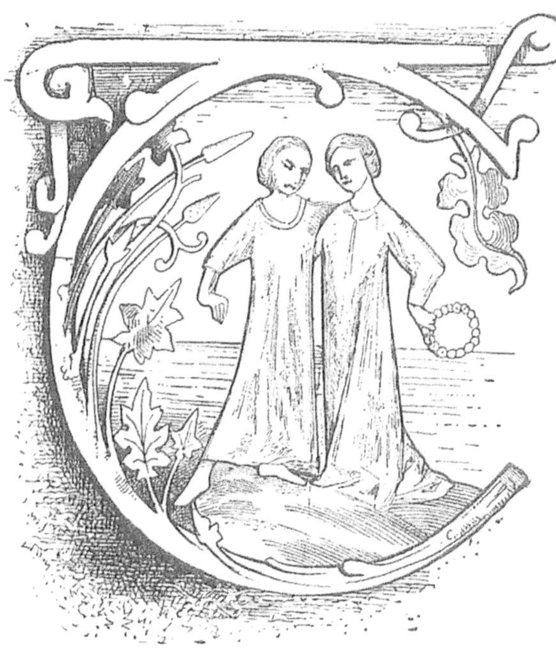

HERE are several small effects in ornament which the carver should study with care; they are generally applicable to most kinds of decorative art. The first of these is the employment of bosses or knobs, some left plain, and some carved, hemispherical or less. They may be almost flat, but are always smooth at the edge and polished. They were very extensively used in early carving and metal-work, and the reader may see many illustrations of them in the works of Hulme. Sometimes the knob becomes a small spot or a mere dot, employed to introduce light into a dark ground. The practical theory is that the knob represents the plain or ornamental head of a nail used to hold the work to the wall, or the rivets of armour, which the Goths transferred from coats of mail to linen and woollen. But the real reason is to introduce points of light.

Knobs or bosses may be placed wherever there are wide spaces between patterns. The rule of employing them is either a few large points or many small ones; they must, however, be used sparingly. The principle of introducing them is of very

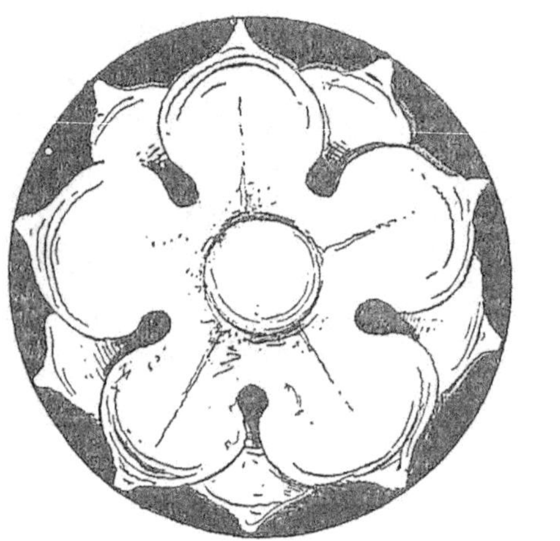

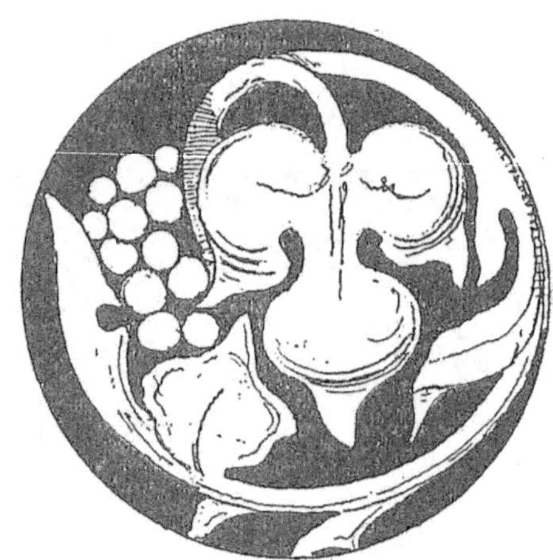

Fig. 59.　　　　　　　　　　　　　　　　Fig. 60.

wide extension. Thus, in all kinds of work, especially metal, grapes, melons, and other fruit are introduced solely that, by their roundness and polish, they may make points of light or " shiners." Old embossed work in leather and wood-carving often owes its chief beauty to the polish, which time and use have given to the reliefs on it. Of course the employment of " shiners " or bosses, and of all kinds of smooth polished relief, should, as a general rule, be sparing, subordinate, and judicious.

Nevertheless, in certain kinds of work, especially in much flat-carving, which is intended to simply ornament a surface, at no great expenditure of labour, just as tiles or tapestry might do, the stems and portions of the leaves, or sometimes all the pattern, may be polished as highly as possible, so as to make a relief against the dark ground. Grounds are pricked or punched or dotted to make them dark, and when the oil soaks into the holes they become permanently darker. Therefore the pattern is to be in contrast ; and when the object is no more

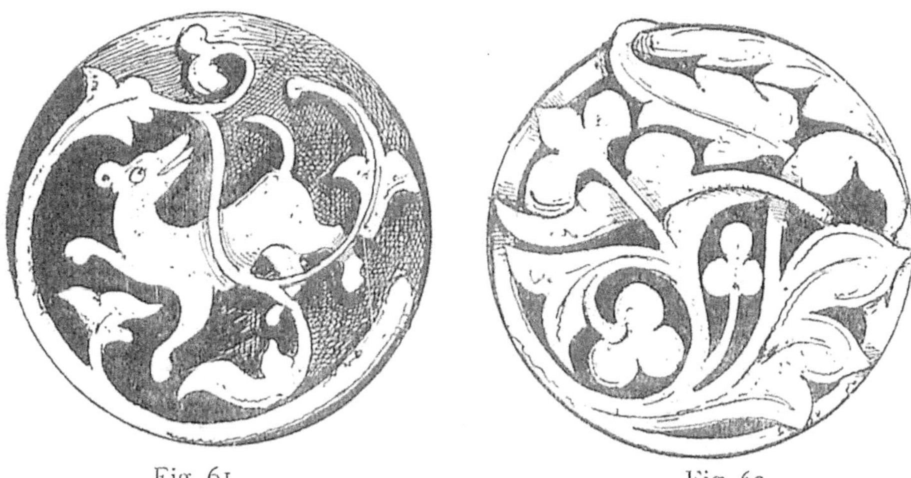

Fig. 61.   Fig. 62.

than to make a general decorative effect, not perfectly finished, but like a sketch, it may be polished.

There is another curious effect given by crossing the pattern alone, or the ground alone, with bars, lines, or stripes. It was very common at one time. In carving, it may be produced with a small gouge or fluter ; though not natural, except where it is given in long and short lines to represent the graining of wood, it has a good effect simply because it distributes shadow evenly. It was probably derived from the effect of " ribs " in cloths, which were much admired by the Venetian painters.

Door-knobs are effectively bosses, that is to say, the same ornamentation may be applied to both, as to handles for bureaus, cabinets, and other furniture. Figs. 59 to 62 will give the pupil some examples and ideas for carving knobs and bosses.

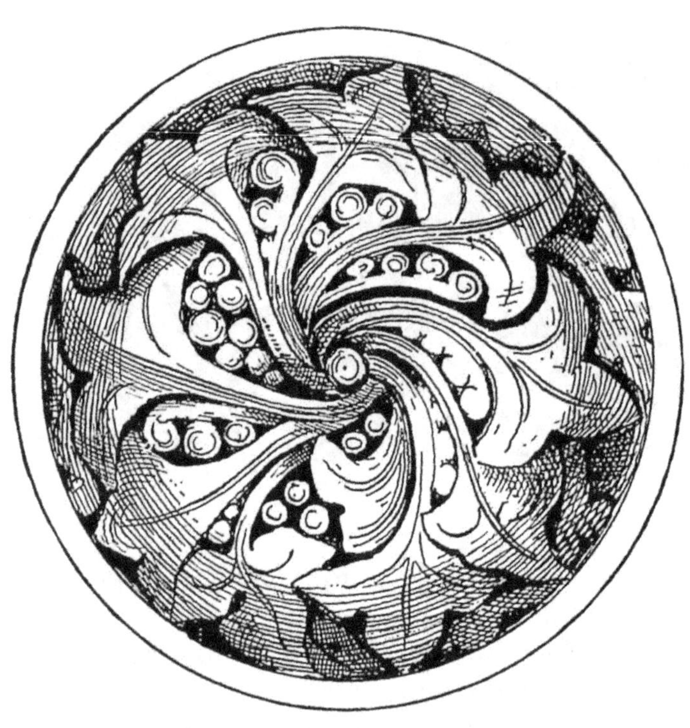

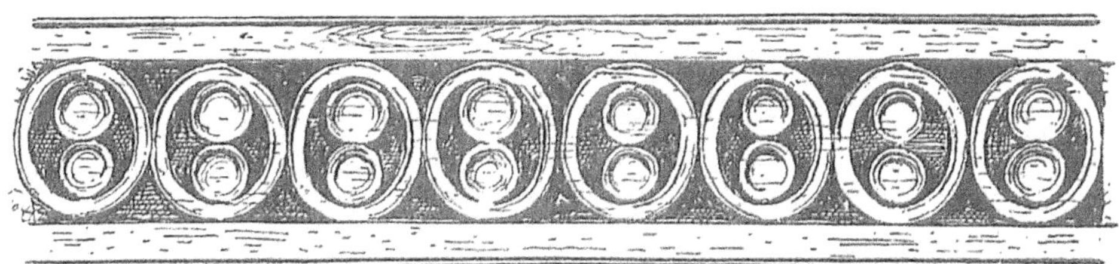

SEVENTEENTH LESSON.

TO REPAIR WOOD-CARVING—GLUE—NITRIC ACID GLUE—
PREPARING DECAYED WOOD—ARTIFICIAL WOOD—
FILLERS—SPRAYING—TO MAKE GLUE "TAKE."

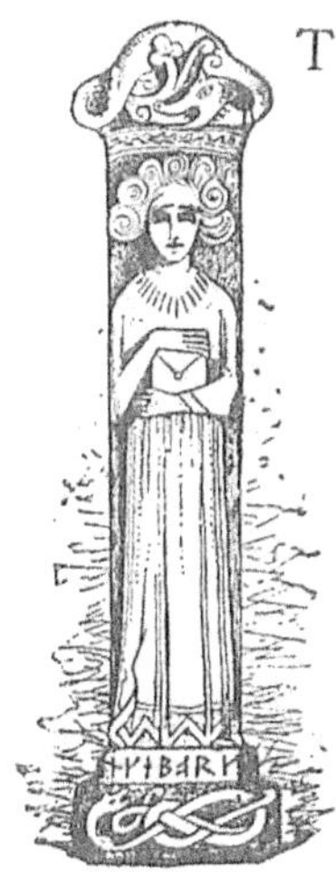

T will sometimes happen to a carver that, owing to bad wood or inadvertence, he splits away or breaks off a piece from his work. In this case he must have recourse to glue. This should be of the very best quality, perfectly light and clean. Glue is made in what alchemists used to call a *balneum mariæ*, that is, of a vessel containing hot water, within which is a smaller vessel. The glue, which is in the inner pot, is therefore to be boiled by the heat of warm water, and not of the fire directly. Before setting it to boil, break it into very small pieces, say of the size of a hazel nut, and let it stand in cold water for twelve hours. It will now be like a thick jelly. Pour off all the water not absorbed, and put the jelly into the inner pot, fill the outer with water and let it boil till the glue is like a thick cream. Use it while in this state.

If you add to the glue, while thus liquid, some nitric acid, say about a tea-spoonful to half a pint of glue, you will have a very superior cement, which holds faster than the plain glue, and is much less liable to crack or split. It dries more slowly, which makes it very valuable for veneering and for large surfaces, where glue often dries before the whole can be applied. Again, when an article fastened with common glue is detached, it is often almost impossible to stick it on again with the same. But with the acidulated glue this is easy.

The greatest advantage of this glue is, that if it be kept excluded from the air it will remain in a liquid state for at least a year, and can be used cold. Its disadvantages are a very pungent and not agreeable smell, and the fact that, when corked up, the cork is most certain to get glued to the bottle, and requires to be broken to get it out, rendering a new one necessary. This may be avoided, however, with great care. Stir the acid into the glue with a glass rod or tube.

It may happen that a rotten, broken place is found even in the best wood; or the carver may obtain possession of a piece of ancient, worm-eaten, half-decayed carving, and with a very little skill such pieces can be perfectly repaired. Take a piece of similar wood, and reduce it to fine sawdust by means of a rasp. For this purpose American walnut and dark old oak, or cocoa-nut shell, which is easily pulverized in a mortar, is excellent. Make this into a paste with glue, and repair with it any broken places. This, if properly made, is quite like wood itself, and may be moulded into any shape. It "takes hold" of the ground, and when dry it may be filed into uniformity with the rest. It may also be cut with ease or trimmed to shape, or, in fact, carved. If there is too little glue in it it will break too easily, if there is too much it will be too glazy. But a proper mixture makes it quite like wood.

Scratches and chance cuts may be remedied by merely melting them with hot water. But for such small defects a *filler* is useful.

This is a kind of paint or liquid cement, the object of which is to fill up the pores of certain coarse woods and make the surface fine. The squeezing wax, described in the chapter on making moulds, is a filler. Others are made by mixing flour with varnish, etc. Any dealer in paints and varnishes will supply a filler suitable to any special work.

When a piece of wood-work is so decayed that it is absolutely dropping to pieces, and cannot even be handled, it may be preserved and rehabilitated by the following process. Take some thin glue and water, or mucilage, or size of any kind, and a *spray*, that is, one of those articles such as are used for spraying perfumes, etc., and which are for sale in most chemist's shops. Spray or sprinkle the glue over the figure, and, if necessary, gradually throw on it fine sawdust or other powder. As it dries it may be shaped and worked more freely.

We read continually in the newspapers of the opening of old tombs and ancient subterranean caves, in which are discovered dead bodies, bones, dresses, implements of bone and wood or leather, or even of baked earth, which gradually dropped into dust a few hours after being exposed to the air. And I have never known a case in which these objects could not have been preserved ; certainly all which I have ever seen could have been. All that is necessary to do is to make a thin size, and very gradually spraying or sprinkling it on the objects, allow it to dry, little by little. There are very few cases in which, indeed, the spray cannot be successfully used. It was by the application of this principle that Sir Joseph Hooker preserved the ivory articles brought from Nineveh by Sir Austen H. Layard, and which would have perished but for him. He advised that they should be boiled in gelatine. The student who becomes an expert in such repairing will find plenty to do, and it will be his own fault if it is not profitable. Nineteen people out of twenty have not the least conception of the degree to which repairs may be carried. Some years ago a gentleman in America had a very curious and valuable vase from the pyramid of Cholula in Mexico. It was very fragile, being made of the weakest terra-cotta, and having been broken to pieces, the owner was about to throw it away, but gave it to me. Some months after I repaired it so perfectly that the closest observation could not detect a flaw in it. I did this by fastening pieces of paper on the inside with gum, and so gradually bringing the fragments together, edge to edge, and fastening them with the acidulated glue. When all were together, there was, of course, a lining of paper. Where there was a fault or a deficiency outside, I filled it in with plaster of Paris, rubbed it all even, and coloured by "rubbing in" paint. This process would have been much easier with decayed wood.

In gluing ordinary wood together, heat the two pieces first. This renders them more inclined to "take" the glue. Some-times it is a difficult thing to hold them together till they "set," that is, adhere so firmly that they will hold. For this the clamp, Fig. 7a, may often be used. In other cases, take two pieces of wood, put one on each side of the parts to be glued, and tie them tightly together; sometimes clamps may be used to connect the binding pieces, when they are not applicable to what is to be glued. Strong indiarubber rings or gummed paper strips may be used in some cases. But with thought, ingenuity can generally be awakened so as to help one out of any such difficulty.

A very perfect resemblance to carved wood may be made by taking cocoa-nut powder or fine sawdust and mixing it with the acidulated glue, so as to make a paste as already described. Then, having ready a mould, either of plaster of Paris or of sunk or incised wood, and oiling it, take the impression. These casts, retouched and glass-papered, are quite like wood, and they may be used for decoration in doors.

The following are also excellent recipes for glue.

Liquid glue. Take of best glue three parts, place them in eight parts of water, allow them to soak for some hours. Take half a part of hydrochloric acid (muriatic acid), three-quarters of a part of sulphate of zinc, add to these the glue, and keep the whole at a moderately high temperature till fluid.

Exceedingly strong cement for glass and china. Take gum arabic and dissolve it in acetic acid instead of water. It must be melted in a hottish place ; it will be much stronger if this be done. The finest quality of sheet gelatine makes a transparent glue.

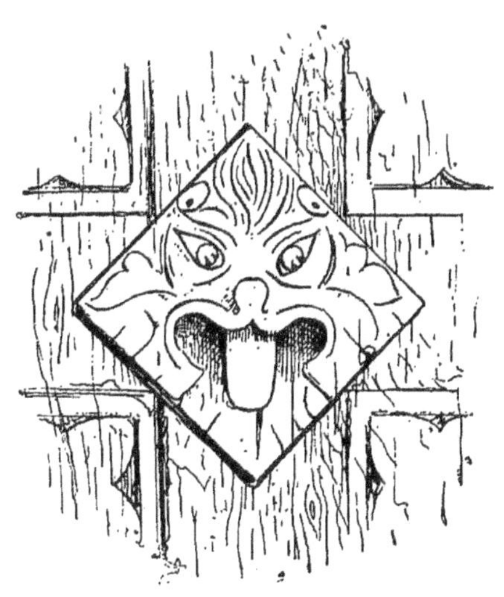

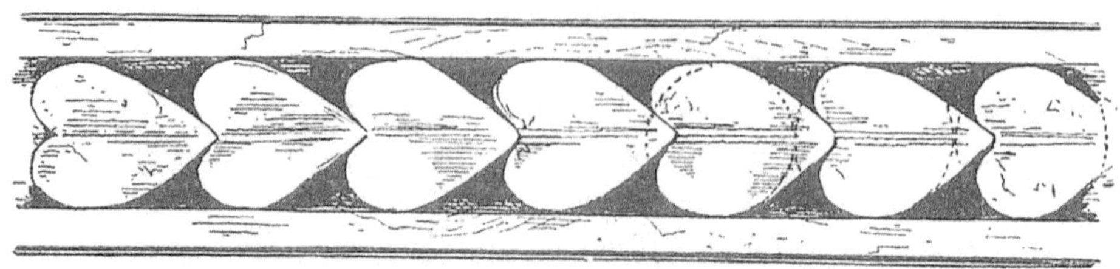

EIGHTEENTH LESSON.

COLOURING WOOD-WORK—OILING—SODA—STAINS AND DYES—IVORYING SURFACES—BLACK DYES AND INK.

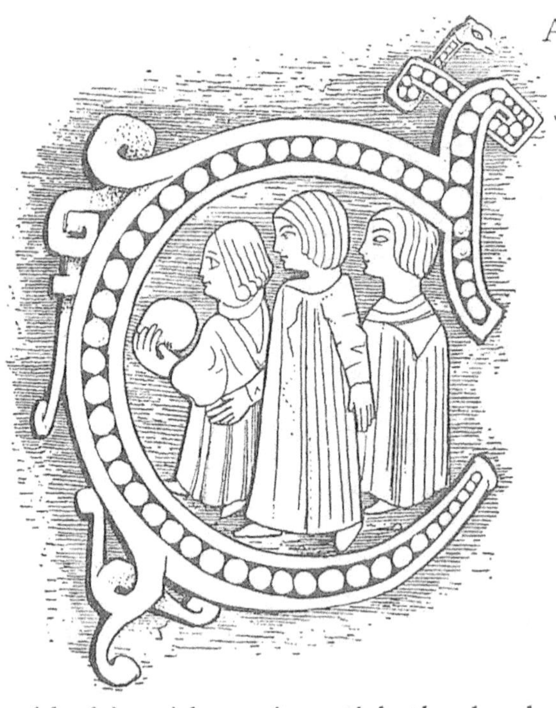

ARVED or any other wood is often dyed, stained, or toned. Sometimes this is done to make one piece or part match with another ; or it may be to imitate the effect of age, or to give light woods a colour which will prevent them from showing defects. This is effected in many ways.

Oiling alone is a kind of colouring, for all oiled wood becomes much darker before long. The more frequently it is rubbed in with a pine stick the harder and darker the surface becomes. I have seen walnut tables which had been thus rubbed with a stick or a hard scrubbing brush, until a tea-cup wet with hot water on the outside would make no mark on them. Had they been only softly oiled or painted, or varnished, an indelible stain must have resulted. Care should be taken that the oil is pure, and that *no wax* has been boiled in it. A table which has had wax on it for a polish will always show marks or stains from hot water.

Soda dissolved in water, and applied to oak with a sponge or brush, will give it a darker tone, which may be increased by several applications. Dark tea with a little alum is also useful, also porter or beer, also a decoction of walnut leaves. In America butternut gives a very rich indelible dye. Let it be carefully observed that in using these, or any other colours, the following rules must be strictly observed. I. Use a sponge or brush and do not apply the dye profusely or pour it on, as you will run great risk of warping the wood, or causing it to split. II. It may be advisable to dry it near a fire, but in this case exercise great care that the heat be not too great. III. When dry, rub the dye off with a rag or soft old newspaper, or chamois skin. Do this very carefully, and do not be disappointed if it seem very light and to have taken but little dye. Apply the dye again, giving it plenty of time to dry between the coatings. Of course this depends on the dyes used, and the degree of colour required.

Stephens' stains of different kinds, to imitate all kinds of wood, or those of *Mander* (Oxford Street, London), are very good, and may now be purchased in every town. As a rule, most of these dyes are very strong, and it is therefore necessary to dilute them with water and make several applications, instead of putting on the whole strength at once. The diluted dye is carefully painted over the entire surface with a full flat camel's hair brush, and a smaller round brush is used in the corners and smaller recesses. After using dyes, and when perfectly dry, the wood should be oiled.

Ammonia. Wood, and especially oak, may be not only stained of a very dark rich colour, giving the effect of age, by washing it carefully with ammonia or spirits of hartshorn, and then exposing it for some time in a chimney, or otherwise to the fumes of smoke, especially of a wood-fire if it be possible. Strong spirits of ammonia, according to Rowe, may be placed in an open vessel and then shut up with the panel in an air-tight chamber or box, the wood darkening according to the length of time it is left in. The ammonia may have to be renewed, as it quickly evaporates. For small work a glass shade may be used, or a box can be made with a glass lid, and after the panel and saucer of ammonia have been placed inside, the crevices can be pasted over with brown paper. When the depth of colour is obtained, which can be seen through the glass, the panel can be taken out. The wood must be so placed that the ammonia can pass quite round the parts which require darkening. But for ordinary purposes, it will be found quite sufficient to apply strong ammonia with a brush or sponge, and expose it to smoke.

Umber. Common powdered umber, which is used by the house painter, is much preferable to the Swiss brown liquid stain to produce an antique brown appearance. The Swiss dye is entirely too rich and uniform, making everything exactly alike, or similar to chocolate. But the umber must be properly applied. Mix it with beer or porter ; strong coffee is also very good ; and apply it with a brush. When dry rub it very carefully, clean, and apply it again. If it be desirable to make the wood very dark, add lamp-black to the dye, mixing and shaking it very thoroughly. But always let the first applications be of umber alone. By adding the lamp-black one can darken the wood almost to blackness, and if it be very carefully done, and not in a hurry, and exposed at intervals to smoke in a warm place, a colour second to none may be thus given.

Paint. Wood which is to be exposed to the air must of course be painted in the ordinary way. But there is another method of applying oil paint which is not so generally known or practised, yet which gives very good results. This consists of *rubbing* paint with the hand into wood or on plaster of Paris, papier-maché, or stone. As it is much thinner than with coats laid on with a brush, it appears more like an innate or natural colour. This was the finger painting of the old Venetian artists. The appearance thus produced, when it is skilfully done, is very different indeed from that of an ordinary coat of paint, and in most cases it is much more attractive.

Ivorying. Take a panel, the pattern may be carved, or even produced in the lowest relief by simply indenting the outline with a wheel or tracer. Any degree of relief will, however, do just as well. Apply a coat of thick ordinary copal varnish. When perfectly dry smooth it with finest glass or emery-paper. Then apply the paint; two or three coats are better than one. See that the last is perfectly smooth. Then work on the dry surface with tracer and stamps, as you would on wood or brass. When finished, take a very small fitch-brush and paint Vandyke brown into all the dots, lines, scratches, and irregularities. Let there be a dark line of brown close to the outline of the pattern. Sometimes the entire ground may be *rubbed* with brown, allowing an indication or a few dots of white yellow to show here and there. When dry give two coats of retouching varnish (that of Söhnee Fréres, No. 19, Rue des Filles du Calvaire, Paris, is specially suited to this work). By using olive, dark and light greens, a beautiful imitation of bronze can be thus obtained. In fact, by studying the effects of colour in many kinds of old objects, we may obtain hints for converting very ordinary wood-carving into beautiful objects.

Bichromate of Potash, diluted with water to the required shade, is a good dark dye, but great care should be taken not to spill a drop of it on the clothing, or to get it on the hands, or even to inhale its fumes, as it is a poison.   Apply it with a brush.

Black Dyes. Of late years black dyes have been so much improved that ebony is imitated with holly, hickory, and beech, to absolute perfection.   The best way for the carver, as regards these and all kinds of dyes, such as red, yellow, green, etc., is to go to a chemist or colourman, who will obtain them for him. For black the following recipes may be used.

I.

White vinegar	1 pint.
Iron filings	2 ounces.
Antimony (powdered)	2 ounces.
Vitriol.	1 ounce.
Logwood.	3 ounces.

Steep it in a corked bottle for eight days.

II.

Gall nuts coarsely broken	2 ounces.
Rain water	1 quart.

Boil down to one half.   (*Seaton.*)

To stain wood, first apply No. II., when nearly dry put on No. I. and then No. II. again.   It will occur to the reader that this is really ink, and, in fact, if he cannot get a stain, good common ink applied a few times and well dried will answer quite as well.   After it has been thoroughly put on, and quite dry, oil the surface, and rub it well, and it will be found that it will not wash off from any casual application of water.   Some of the writing inks now made are intensely black and almost indelible.

NINETEENTH LESSON.

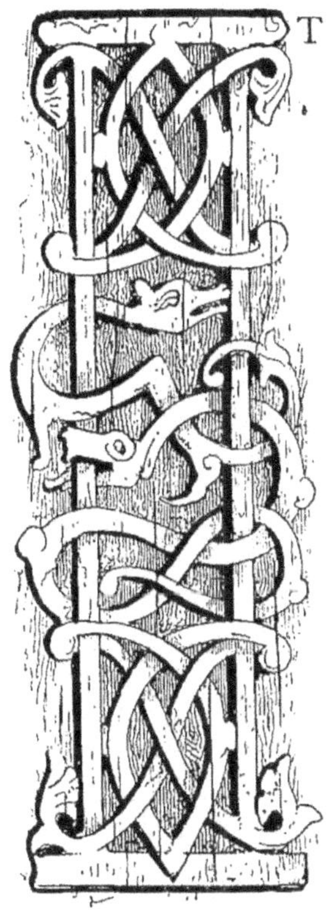

T will very soon become apparent to every wood-carver that it is easier to copy from a model than a drawing, and that this ease is very much increased when he has made that model in clay himself. However, it is also very advisable that he shall, after a time, practise carving from drawings and sketches also, as this of itself gives great skill and accuracy of perception. But he will very often need or wish to have copies of carvings or casts, and these he may obtain with ease, if the relief be not too great or the object too large. This is called "taking a squeeze," and it may be done in two ways. Firstly, by means of squeezing or modelling wax, which is sold by dealers in artists' materials. The use of this and the casting in plaster of Paris is, however, generally tiresome to beginners in carving. For all practical purposes squeezes in paper are quite sufficient.

Paper squeezes. Take any pieces of soft newspaper. Oil the wood or plaster cast which you wish to copy ; soak, and then press on the paper and, with your fingers and a sponge or a very stiff brush, poke and squeeze it into every cranny of the original. If this be done *thoroughly*, the hardest part of the work is accomplished. Now give the paper a brush of flour-paste or gum or mucilage, or paste strengthened with glue, and press on new pieces of paper. To merely copy the original, a few thicknesses will suffice. Take the squeeze off and let it dry; if necessary, touch it up with colour. For this the first coat should be of *white* paper. To make a cast, keep adding paper till the whole is at least half an inch in thickness. Press it as hard as you can while forming the mould. When it is dry you can paint or rub the inside with any dry powder, such as whiting, or varnish it, and then make a cast with the same material, *i.e.* paper and paste, or with plaster of Paris. Papier-maché casts, when rubbed by hand with brown paint, form perfect facsimiles of old wood-work. Rubbed with bronze-powders they resemble metals, or they may be ivoried, by the process described in the chapter on dyes.

Plaster-casts are very easily broken, and are heavy and difficult to transport. Wax is spoiled almost by a touch, and it readily yields to heat. Papier-maché, when properly managed, with a little practice gives a mould which is equal to either for all surfaces except the most minutely delicate. When dry, such casts may be let fall, or really thrown about, without sustaining any injury, and they are very portable. It is very often possible to easily copy an object with paper when plaster or wax cannot be used at all. The reason why it is not more generally used is because few persons have taken the pains to treat it as a plastic material suitable to the arts, or are sufficiently practised in it to know what can really be done with it. The wood-carver should do this, because it is a very important thing for him to keep copies of his works, or to get those of others to use in his designs. With a little practice, and at no expense, he can make such casts in a material which is almost as durable as wood itself.

In large manufactories of papier-maché the pulp of paper is simply mixed with the paste or size, and put into the moulds in large masses, and then subjected to pressure. When a good surface is secured with fine white paper, it is not of much con-sequence how coarse the paper for the *backing* may be. For this purpose it may be mixed with tow or fibre of any kind, plaster, or fine sawdust, etc., so long as the *binder* or size be only strong enough to hold all together. But for all ordinary purposes waste-paper and paste, thickened with common glue, will suffice.

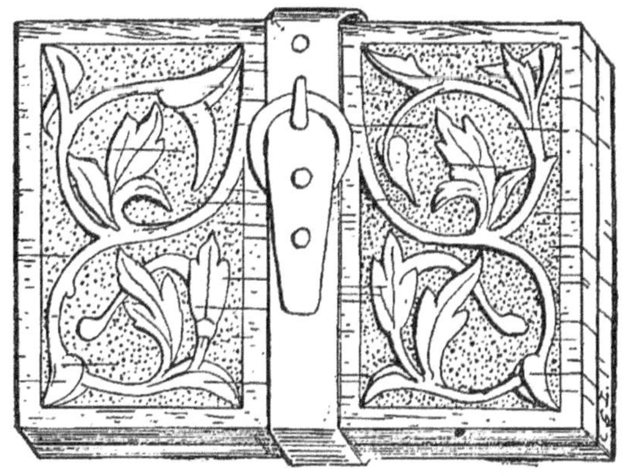

CASE FOR PAPERS OR MUSIC.

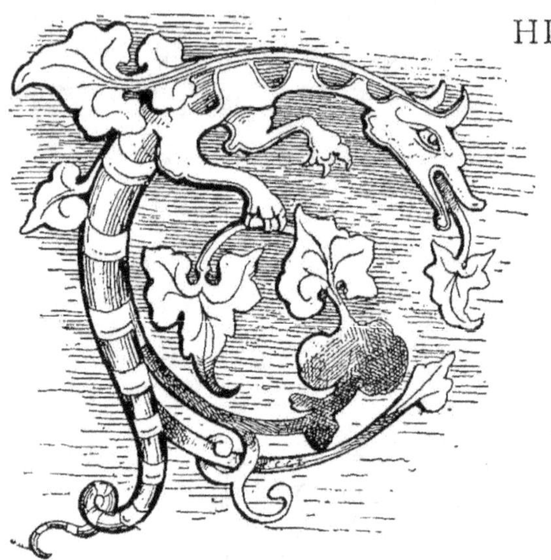

HIS is a manner of ornamenting which can hardly be called carving, and which would not deserve special mention were it not that it is so extensively used, it being the chief method of decoration in all the islands of the Pacific, and still extensively practised in Sweden and Norway. It consists of small incised triangles, or " diamonds," made with a skew or ordinary chisel, which are arranged in rows or lines. Simple as the work may seem, it is very effective when artistically employed ; and it has this peculiarity, that no other kind of cutting is so well adapted, with very little labour, to relieve flat surfaces, such as paddles, tankards, spoons, war clubs, and scoops or dippers.

The triangular incision is made with three cuts ; by adding two more from the opposite direction we make a diamond, or the latter may be produced at once with only four cuts, Fig. 63. To these we may add the hemi-spherical or cup hollow, which is made with a gouge, and which, in Scotland at least, seems to have been the earliest pre-historic beginning of ornamentation of flat surfaces.

When these triangles and diamonds are tastefully arranged in lines, and filled in with a composition, or paint, which contrasts in colour with the wood, the effect is often excellent. Ordinary putty, into which a little mastic has been well worked, or plaster of Paris with size and a little flour paste, with one drop of oil to an ounce, makes a good filler for such a purpose. This may be applied to any incised cutting. An ivory-like filling, which may

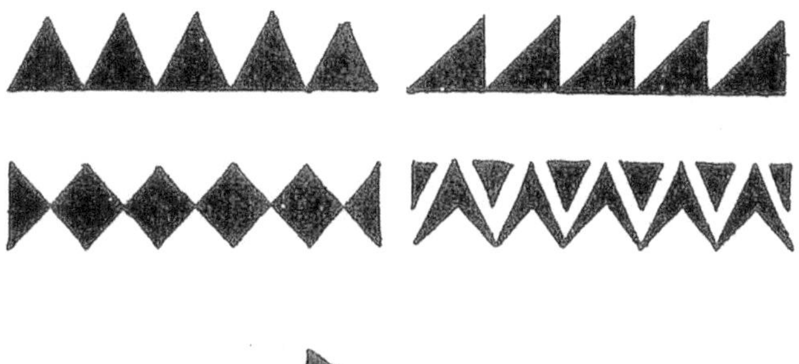

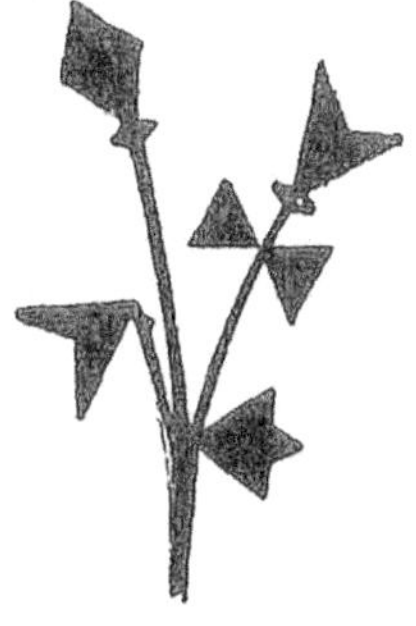

Fig. 63.

be stained of any colour, and which was once extensively used in Florence, is made with rice, lime, and size.

Any pattern which can be drawn in lines may be executed with good effect in triangular spots, the base of every spot being on the line. They may either join one another or be separated ; both methods produce a good effect. The spots may be of all sizes, and are generally not larger than those at the top in the above illustration.

Large triangles may of course be used as well as small ones. Owing to the ease with which these spots are made, and the good effect which they produce when blackened, it is not remarkable that so simple a method of decorating wood is extensively practised.

By placing a gouge vertically and turning it, as already mentioned, a cup-like cavity is easily cut. A row of these is often very effective.

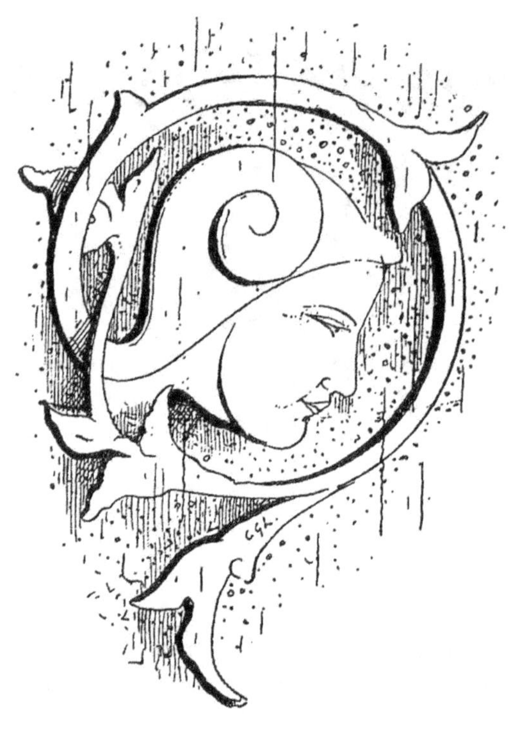

APPENDIX.

OBJECTS FOR WOOD-CARVING.

" The most difficult part of making is to know what to make."

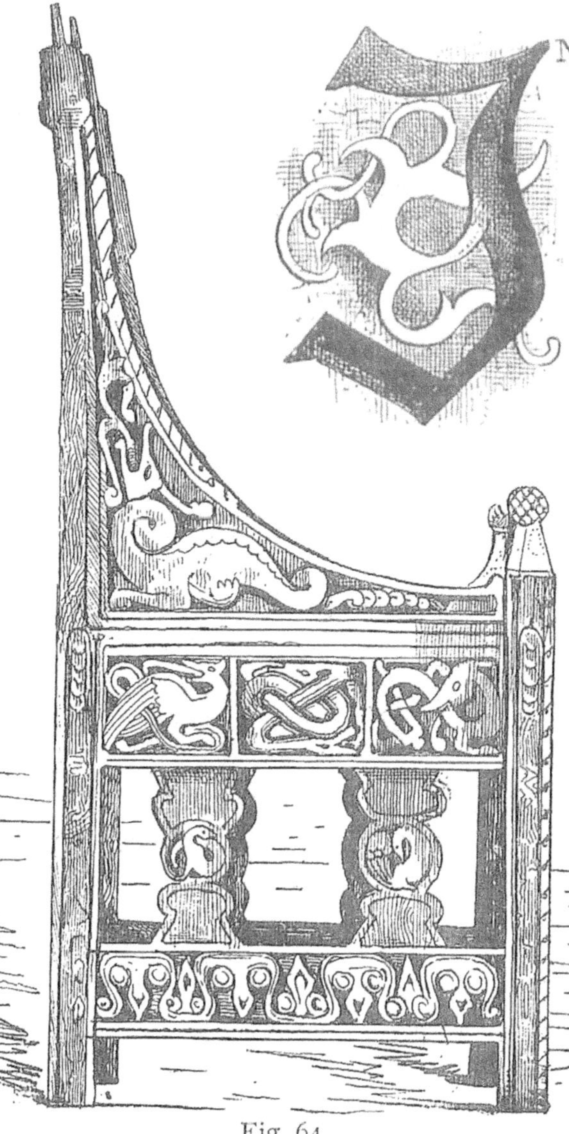

Fig. 64.

N no circumstances should the wood-carver be at a loss for a subject to work on, yet this is the commonest source of complaint, especially among young artists, that they "do not know what to take up." One result of this is the wearisome production of panels or "fancy pieces" without any definite aim, and a constant imitation of one another's work. Unfortunately there are a great many who cannot understand or form any idea how a pattern would look when executed. They will pass it over in an engraving, but when they see it actually carved and made up they appreciate it. Now the tutor should teach the pupils, and the students teach themselves, to think of subjects, to invent them, to sketch and execute them. I have found that all workers are invariably more defective in this respect than in any other, and that it is one in which the direction of almost every art school in the world is either utterly wanting, or else leaves much to be desired.

Pupils should be encouraged to look at every object with an eye to ornamenting or decorating it, so far as that can be done without detracting from its usefulness. In every school a list of objects for carving should be hung up, and the workers be frequently requested to think of subjects to add to the list; outline sketches of furniture and other objects should be supplied. It is not at all understood that even a very little frequent employment of the mind inventing and planning, no matter at what, stimulates *all* the mental faculties to an extra-ordinary degree.

I therefore seriously urge that the wood-carver shall earnestly study the following list of subjects, add to it, and at times take one or the other of them and sketch it with variations. He may remember while doing this, that any of the ornaments given may be varied and applied to different things, as, for instance, the vine on a circular panel may be easily adapted to a square. Full directions for doing this may be found in " The Manual of Design,"[1] price one shilling, which also contains many patterns perfectly adapted to carving.

The first subject to be considered is: What to design or make; how its surface can be appropriately ornamented; and, how to produce the best effect with the least work. Mere elaboration is admired only by the ignorant, and the less cultivated a pupil is, the more inclined he will be to densely crowded petty patterns.

If the pupil wants a design for any of the objects described in this chapter, and if he can draw at all, and has any skill in

[1] London : Whittaker and Co.   Chicago : Rand, McNally and Co.

adapting or changing a pattern, as, for instance, to make one which fills a triangle or a square "set" into a circle, or extend to a long panel or a border, he will find something for any of them, either in this book, or in the "Manual of Design" already referred to. Let him also take pains to collect as many patterns as he can of all kinds, and keep them in a portfolio for reference.

Every student of wood-carving should remember that if he has a folding looking-glass, which he can make for himself by cutting in two a square mirror of, say, six inches by twelve, he can, out of any pattern in this book, or from any simple ornament whatever, make (with the least effort of ingenuity or adaptiveness) a border by repeating it in succession, or a centre ornament which may be multiplied in whole or in part *ad infinitum*. That is to say, he can fill any given space, be it a panel, ceiling, circle, triangle, or hexagon. Or he can fill such spaces by simply cutting out ornaments from card-board, and placing them together to form vines or outgrowths from one another.

Panels. A panel is defined as a board with a surrounding frame. The word is derived from the old English *panel*, a piece of cloth, Latin *pannus*, "a cloth or patch"; from the same word we have *pane*. In wood-carving we practically apply it to small boards intended to be set in furniture, or walls, or ceilings, or made into book-covers or box-lids. The uses of panels are without limit, as they may be introduced into almost every kind of furniture, such as the backs and sides of chairs, chests, bedsteads, caskets, window-garden boxes, doors, or wherever a flat surface can be adorned. When surrounded with a frame or several strips of moulding, any panel becomes improved when the outer frame is not overdone. As a rule the border of a panel should be plain, so as to distinctly define or set forth the pattern. For this reason many very ordinary and even rude subjects "come out" or look well when thus "mounted." A series of carved panels makes a beautiful frieze for any room. A good general size for most work is a panel six inches by twelve, more or less, and half an inch thick. In *spacing* a panel for ornament the pupil may begin by making one circle in the centre and one in each corner, so that the five may fill up the whole space. Convert these into a vine and apply ornaments. There are of course endless variations of this principle. (Consult the " Manual of Design.")

Chairs. Take any chair, copy it, and then fill the spaces with ornaments to be carved. Large, square, high-backed, old-fashioned chairs admit of the most panelling, and can be made up by any cabinet-maker or carpenter, *vide* Fig. 69. It is a very good plan to always have such objects made up in pieces, carve them

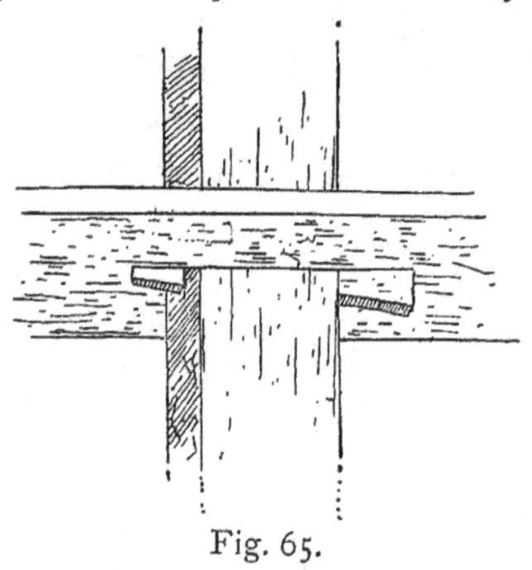

Fig. 65.

separately, and then have them put together. It may be observed for beginners, and those who are not much practised in cabinet-making, that there is a very substantial kind of furniture once made very commonly in Germany, and which has been much revived of late years. It is made entirely without glue, nails, or screws, by simply cutting holes into which tenons or *ends* project, which ends are fastened on the other side by holes and pins.

On this principle every kind of furniture can be made by any man who is ingenious enough to simply measure boards, cut square holes, and adapt pins to them. Such articles as are made by this process are very much stronger than any others, and they have the great advantage that they can be easily taken apart, packed, or be stored in very small space when not in use ; and the style is of course more adapted to carving than ordinary furniture. The writer has in his possession chairs 250 years old made on this principle. The seat is a square nearly two inches thick, in which four holes are bored, into which the legs are simply set, as in a milking-stool. Between the hind legs two square holes are cut, into which similar tenons made in the lower end of the back are fitted. In these tenons two square holes are cut, just exactly on the other side of the seat, into which square pins are driven, Fig. 65. With a very little ingenuity or will, anybody can contrive to make any piece of furniture on the same principle. The seats of chairs and stools, or the faces of tables, should never be carved, for very apparent reasons. There is plenty of space for the carver to work at on the edges and legs, and this may be made striking enough by means of colouring and gilding, Figs. 64 and 66.

Boxes. These have formed in all ages favourite subjects for decoration. They vary from the smallest casket to the chest. A box with the lid forms five panels, or,

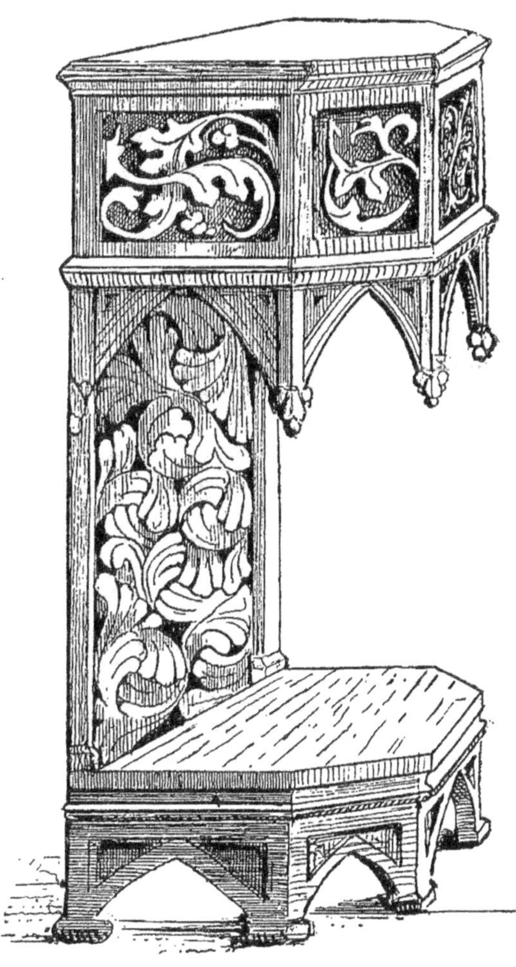

Fig. 66. Console or Bracket.

seen from any point, three.   In Italy, of old, they were often
carved without and within.   Boxes may be made by simply
gluing, nailing, or screwing together, but they may be so
dovetailed by an expert workman that the juncture is quite im-
perceptible.   *Vide* "Forty Lessons in Carpentry Practice," by
C. F. Mitchell.   Cassell and Co.   It is a feat in cabinet-making

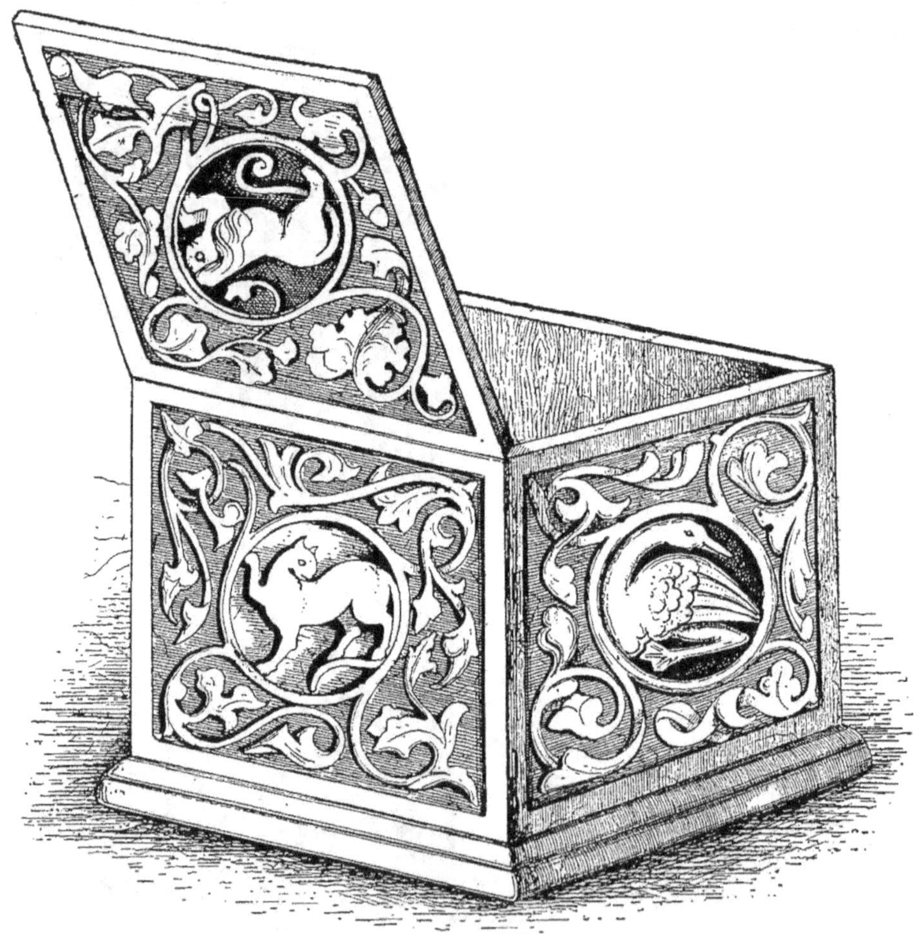

Fig. 67.

to do this *perfectly*, and boxes thus joined are very expensive. The appearance of boxes is much improved by the addition of moulding-strips, bases, and projecting ornaments. The student is advised to carve or buy a few bosses, such as heads of animals or faces, and rosettes, and try the experiment of fitting them to a box or carving them on one, Fig. 67.

Caskets for Cigars. This applies also to receptacles into which glasses for flowers may be put. Take a cylinder of wood, turned, or made up like a barrel, and fit a base to it, and a lid. They may be made of very large joints of bamboo, which may also be beautifully carved, and partly coloured in

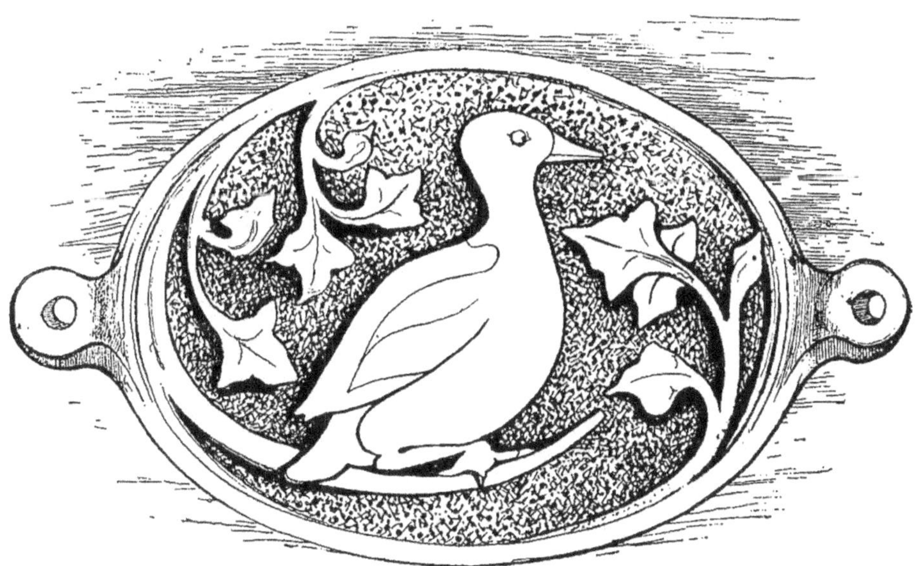

Fig. 68.   TRAY FOR CIGAR ASHES.

the lines, as is common in China. It is best for turned cylinders and bamboo to have them surrounded with metal rings to prevent their splitting. They may also be made square, that is, as boxes.

Trays for Cigar Ashes. These are best when carved from

hard wood, such as box, though any other may be used. It is much better that they be made rather larger and deeper than many in use, as ashes are continually being knocked out of small and shallow ones. They may be round or square, like a fish or a small book (with a lid), a shell, a tortoise, or a scooped hand, a face, or a figure of any animal or human being, Fig. 68.

Basket-work. This is very easily imitated in wood, and it forms a very pretty and fanciful style for many kinds of objects. Take any kind of basket-work, either that of split osiers, which are half-round, or Italian rush-work, or American Indian, which is made of flat strips of ash or pine-bark interwoven, or Indian rattan, and imitate it with flat gouges or firmers. It is very easy work, and beginners soon become expert in it. It improves the effect, when the work is finished, if dark colour be painted into the depressions. Basket-work may be used for diaper ground. The American Indian basket-work, in flat strips from one-third of an inch to an inch in breadth, is easiest to imitate, and may be executed with a single V tool or firmer.

Casks, Small Barrels, Kegs. These are useful for waste-paper boxes, or to contain canes and umbrellas. When carved and coloured they form very attractive articles of furniture. They may be used for garden seats. Heads of animals *appliqué* to these, some for handles to lift them, or else holes must be cut in them for this purpose, *vide* Fig. 56.

Frames for Pictures or Looking-glasses. These give a wide range to the wood-carver, for all borders are suitable to frames. Heads may be *appliqué* to corners and centres of frames. It is very much to be desired that designers and carvers would exert their inventiveness and endeavour to break up the monotony and feebleness which characterize most frames, *vide* borders and photograph frames.

Horns. Horns may be carved, as previously described, and imitations of them in wood are easily made. They are orna-

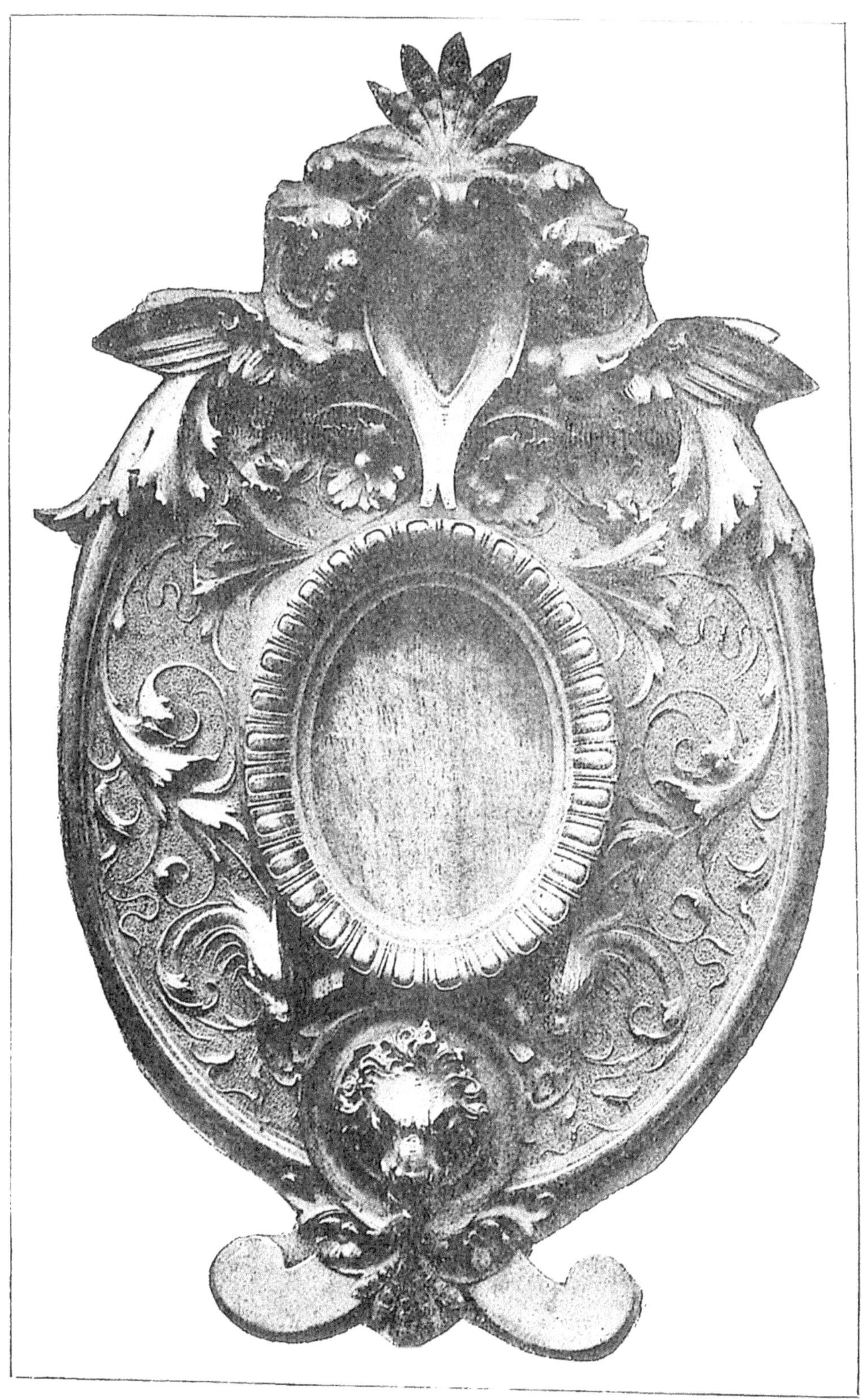

MINIATURE FRAME.

P. 128.

mental objects, and useful when hung up to contain small objects. They can, by steeping in hot water, be softened and flattened, *vide* initial to Fifteenth Lesson.

Tiles. These are really panels. They are pieces of wood from half an inch to an inch in thickness, the size of ordinary tiles, carved in bold relief with free hand, coloured or not, and are very useful for house decoration, chimney-piece borders, cornices, and corners. The tile when employed with much repetition becomes the diaper ornament.

Window Gardens to contain flower-pots. These are square chests, as long as the window is wide, and from a foot to eighteen inches in depth. They may be made with two or three panels, or one long panel in front, with one at each end. They form admirable subjects for decoration.

Albums, Portfolios, Book-covers. These are panels, and afford an infinite range of design and effects in wood-carving. They may be very beautifully and easily ornamented in mere stamping and outlining (*vide* Lesson II.), or by putting in diaper grounds, or basket-work, or by very low relief carving, in which case there should be a border in a little higher relief to protect the pattern from being rubbed, Fig. 70.

Canoes. In many countries large or real canoes are made from one piece of wood and elaborately carved. Very pretty miniature canoes may be made from one to three feet in length from any kind of wood, and covered with any kind of ornamentation. It is not necessary to excavate them from a single block or log, as they may be made from two or more pieces. They form useful receptacles for many objects.

Panels of Doors. These might be generally ornamented. Every kind of wood-carving is applicable to them, but it should be remembered that for all such decoration a large, free, and bold style is absolutely necessary, and that it is unwise to make mural work, which should be visible at great distances, out of

K

pretty flowers or too delicate work. A room with good bold door-panels, wainscot, or dado and a frieze, seems half furnished, while trifling and feeble ornaments detract from such appearance.

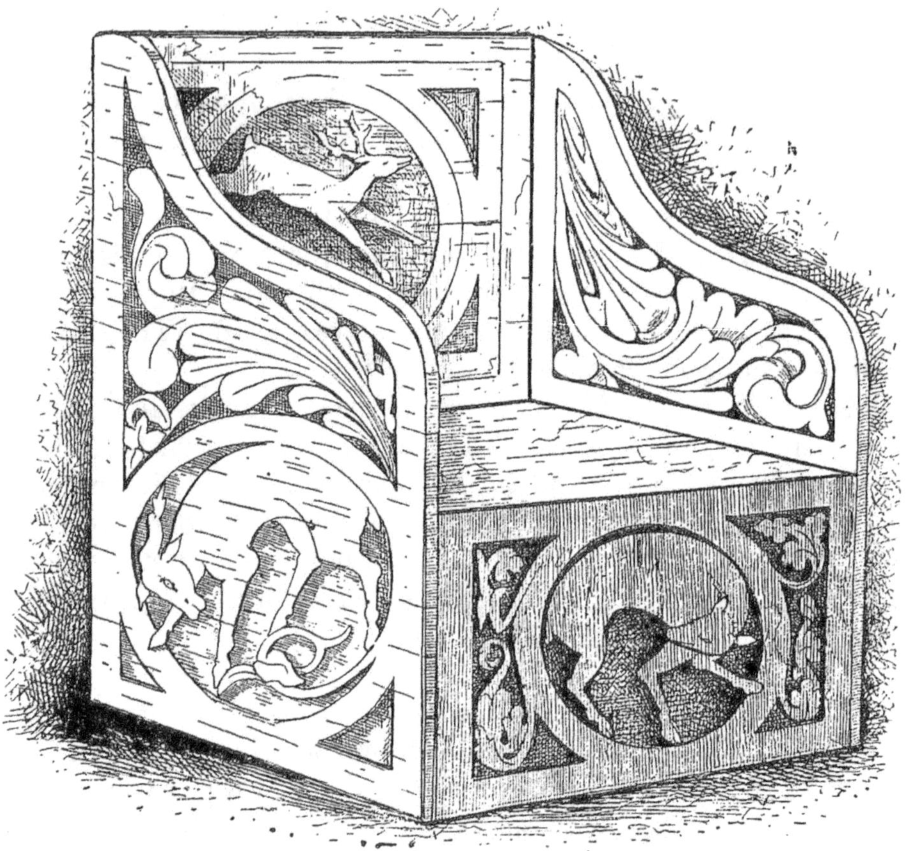

Fig. 69.

The great secret of the attractiveness of mediæval and savage decoration is its energy. Even eccentricity and grotesqueness lose all that is repulsive in them when they are simply and vigorously set forth.

Carved patterns in low relief may be applied to door-panels.

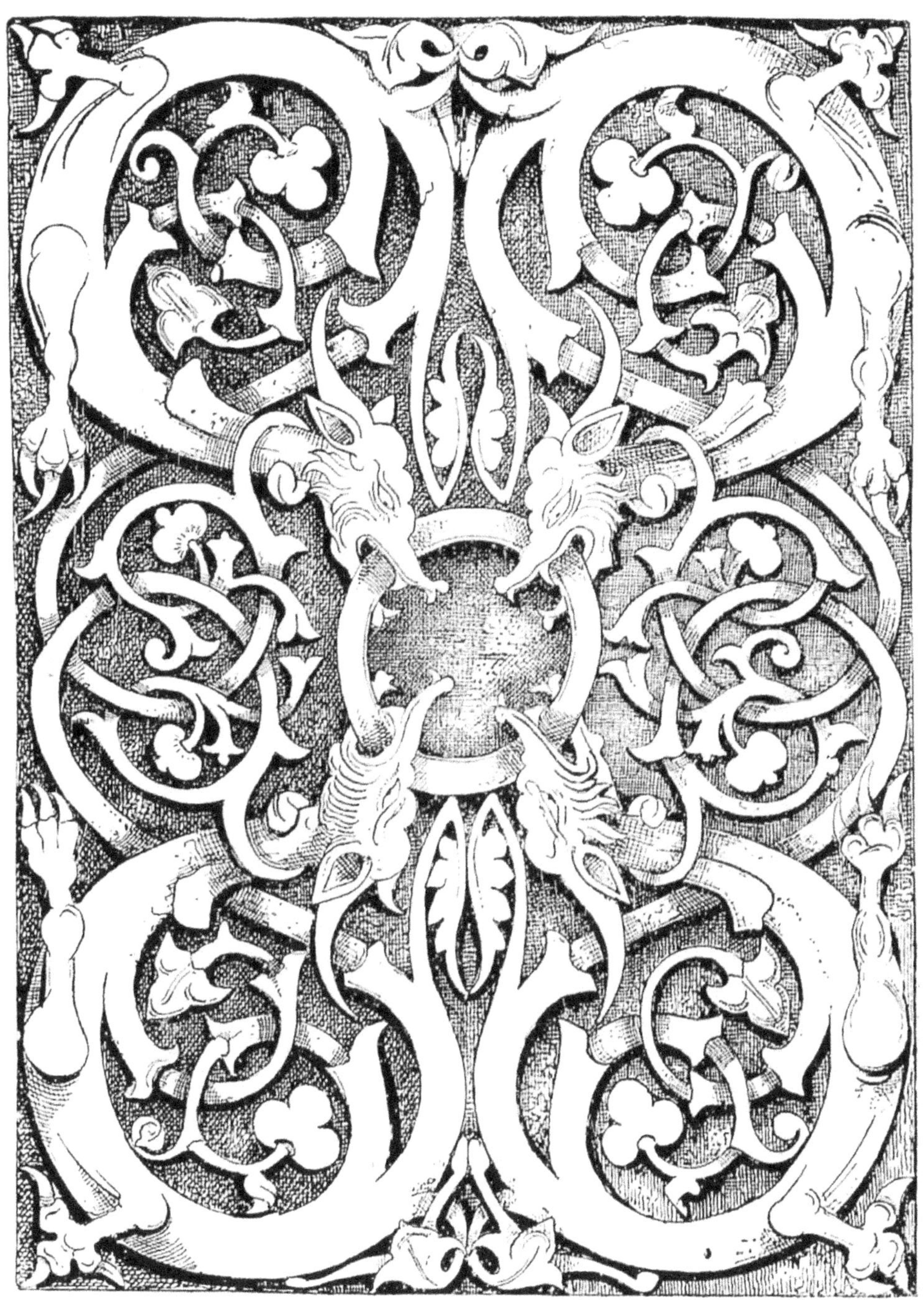

Fig. 70.   ALBUM COVER.

Foot-stools. These are really small panelled boxes, unless made with supports or legs.

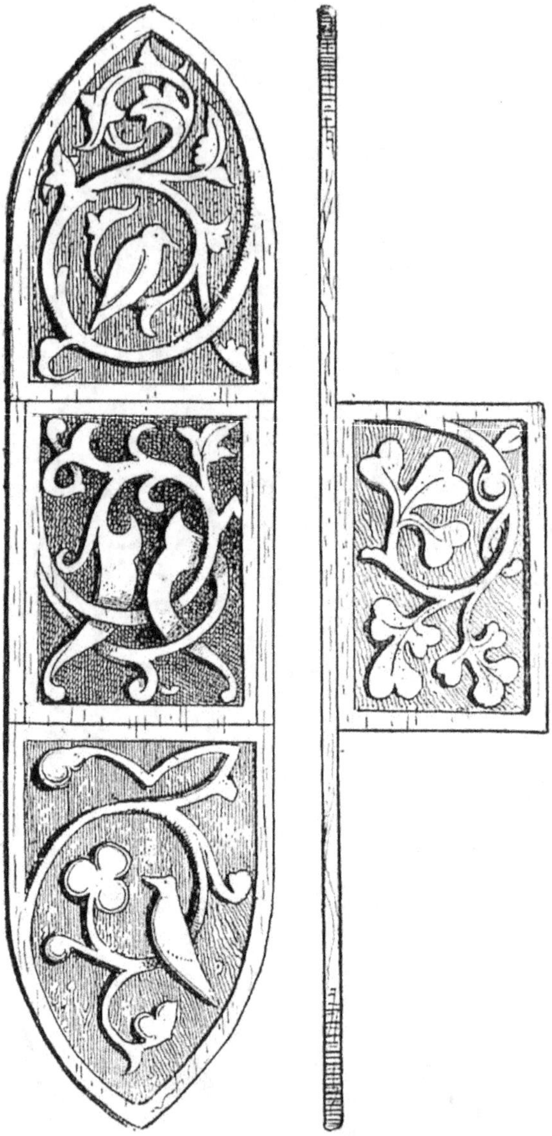

Benches. Simple benches are seldom decorated, but they are admirably adapted to it. Never carve the seats, unless they are made to fold up to protect them from the rain, in which case the under ornaments of choir-seats or misereres may be appropriately used. When the bench has a back it becomes a rude sofa or settee or settle (Anglo - Saxon *setl*, a seat). Properly speaking a settle is a *long* bench with a high back. This may be carved in panels. There was an old Saxon and early English double chair made to seat two, which is like a short settle.

Hanging Boxes. These are boxes generally made with a back, which

Fig. 71.   HANGING BOX.

is the longest piece, and which goes above and below the receptacle part. They are useful for newspapers or letters. Every kind of carving is applicable to them, Fig. 71.

Key Boxes. These are small hanging cabinets. In every family there are many loose keys of trunks and furniture lying about loose, and hard to find when wanted. If there were a key box they would always be readily found. Make a box or frame, let us say eighteen inches in length by ten inches width, of four strips of deal or any wood. These strips may be half an inch in thickness by an inch in width. Nail or glue them together so as to form the four sides of a box. Then take one or two or three strips of thin planed board, and neatly nail them on to form a back to the shallow box. Now take a panel, which is to form the lid or door of the cabinet. It will be better to make a narrow frame of four strips, and set the panel in this, as a door, with hinges and lock. This is to be hung up on the wall. It will very much improve the whole if the interior and outside of the cabinet, or all the deal, be stained to match the door, which, as it is to be carved, should be of walnut or oak, or some better class of wood. Then get some small silver or plated-headed nails and drive them in rows in the cabinet. The keys are to be hung up on these.

Cabinets. These may be in the nature of upright boxes with doors, with three sides ornamented, the fourth being placed against the wall, or three-sided for a corner. The forms of cabinets are extremely varied, and the artist should pass much time in designing them. They are of all sizes, from great *armoires* for clothing down to caskets. The word cabinet is derived from the French *cabane*, a cabin. The earliest dwellers in Italy made the receptacles for the ashes of the dead exactly like the cabins in which they dwelt.

Sabots or Wooden Shoes. These serve admirably to carve, and are very pretty when coloured or ivoried, bronzed in antique style, or otherwise ornamented. Sabots are useful to contain small articles, and may be turned into cigar-ash holders.

Umbrella Handles. These offer an inexhaustible field for the designer and carver of small objects.

Tankards. These and all kinds of cylindrical objects are the same as regards design as panels, only that the pattern when not in set divisions must be continuous, or going round without a break. They have been already described.

Pen and Pencil Boxes. A very convenient form is that of a round-turned wood, plain, upright jar. Small square or round carved boxes for such a purpose are not hard to make. They may be made like towers or castles, the trunks of trees, barrels, or almost any hollow objects.

Pilgrim Bottles and Powder Flasks. Take two pieces of board, each one inch thick, plane them smooth, and saw both into ovals exactly matching, of, say, six inches by ten. Cut away the centre from both.

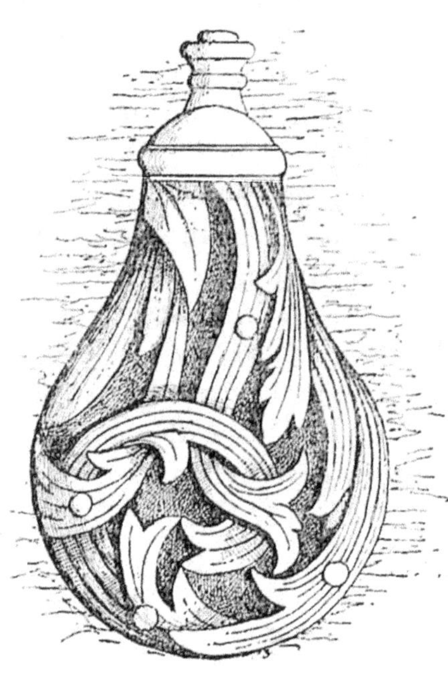

Fig. 72. FLASK.

Fit them exactly. Then round each half in such a manner that, when brought together, they form a round ring, like a French loaf. Then carefully hollow out the centre of both, including the neck, and glue the halves together. Carve the outside, Figs. 72 and 73. During the Middle Ages such bottles were made of many sizes to contain gunpowder. They were carved from ivory or hard wood, and were covered with a very great

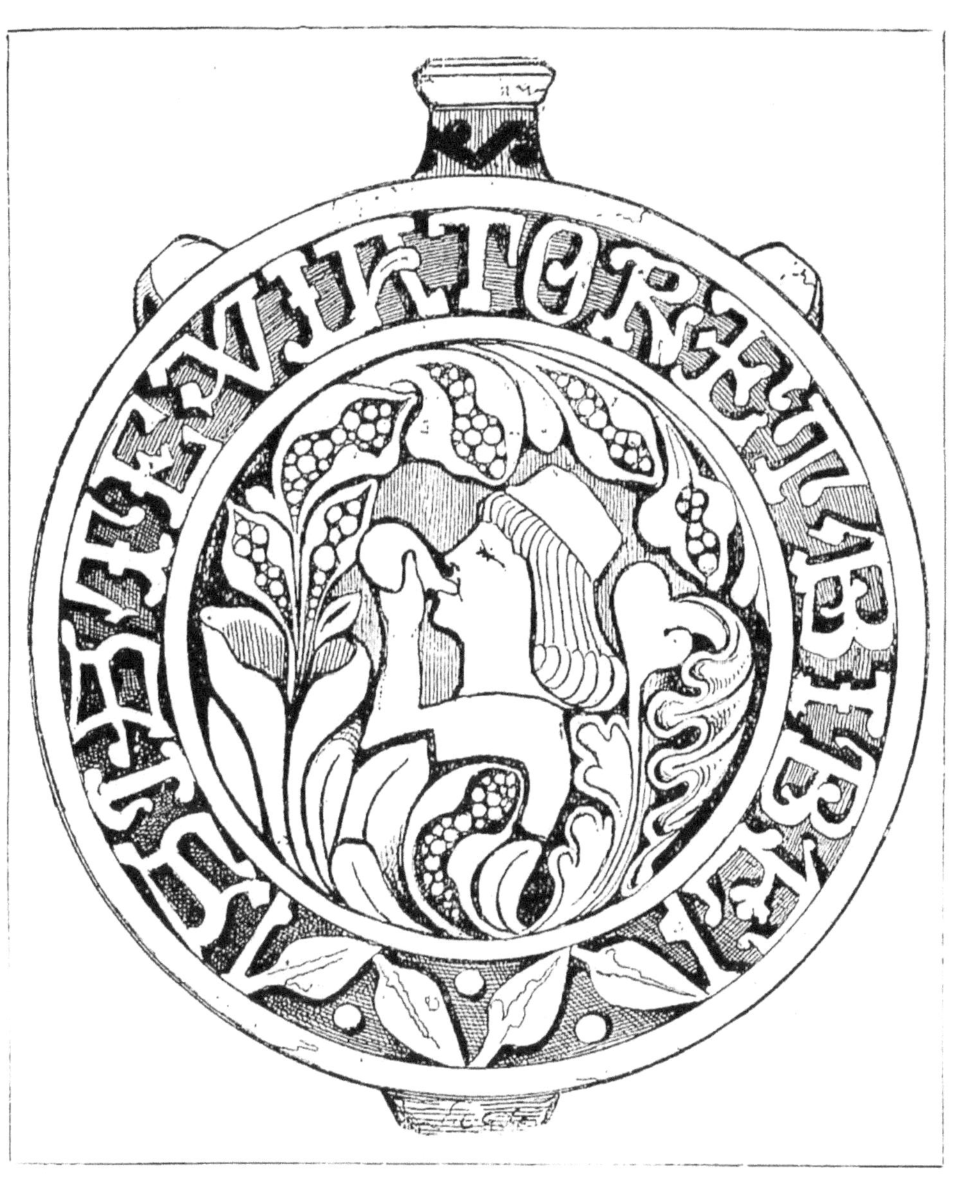

Fig. 73. Pilgrim Bottle.

variety of subjects, such as deer, dogs, wild boars, birds, cupids, scenes from the heathen mythology and the Bible, as well as ordinary grotesques.

Shrines or Reliquaries. This is the conventional name for boxes or caskets made exactly in the form of houses, the lid being one side of the roof. The shape is a convenient one for a box. They were covered with ornaments of the most varied or grotesque kinds.

Mummies. The Egyptian mummy or its outward box or sarcophagus forms an excellent subject for a useful box. Take two pieces of wood, adapt them to make a box, like the Egyptian type, that is, the lid being about one-fourth as thick as the box. *Appliqué* or glue more wood on to the lid, in the centre. The whole may be then smoothed into shape, painted and gilt, or else carved in low relief, or simply stamped. It may also be all gilt, and the dot work and shadows painted in brown or ivoried. Take for model a real sarcophagus. The work is not difficult, and the result will be a very handsome object.

Roman Sarcophagus. This is simply a square box carved in very high relief, after the pattern of a Roman tomb. The ornaments may be *appliqué*. These sarcophagi are very beautiful when ivoried.

Books. A very pretty pattern for a box is an old book of the twelfth or thirteenth century, with its clasps and other ornaments in high relief. One of the covers is set on hinges, and forms the lid. Care should be taken to polish and ornament the whole so as to look like an original. It was very common to make the sides of old books of wooden panels, which were carved in high relief. Silver and brass or iron clasps and studs taken from such old books may be bought in many bric-à-brac shops.

Staves or Alpenstocks. A staff four or five feet in length is more useful for a pedestrian going a great distance than a cane, and it is remarkable that it should have fallen into such disuse.

In old times in northern countries they were often made square, the corners being slightly rounded, and were then covered with Runic inscriptions and ornaments. These were very often almanacks, so that a man wishing to know what was the day of the week or month had only to consult his staff, or to "up stick." These were called clogs. They might be acceptable and useful to many tourists. They were commonly carved by the peasants, and a few may possibly still be found in Suffolk.

Spoons. Wooden spoons are easily carved and ornamented. It is very curious, that quite apart from any modern slang attached to the words "spooney" or "to spoon," two spoons, from their fitting together exactly, are considered in many countries as a type of matrimony and perfect agreement. In Wales, as in Sweden and Algeria, it is usual to present a newly married couple with a piece of wood carved into the form of two spoons, and I myself possess specimens of such. If anyone wishes to establish the custom in England he would probably find that the present would be generally welcome. Two spoons in one cup are, it is well known, the sign of a happy marriage. I have seen large wooden spoons carved and painted and varnished, or gilt ; two of these tied together with a ribbon were hung up as an amulet to secure peace.

Bellows. These are carved in low relief, and may be ornamented by simple indentation or outlining and stamping. It is the easiest course to get the wood and saw it out, half or one-third inch walnut or oak, and then carve it, and have the bellows made up, Figs. 74 and 75.

Platters. Take a piece of panel, one-third to half of an inch in thickness, and saw it out into any shape, such as that of a fish, a wild boar, a pig, a cat, a rabbit, tortoise, hare, etc., care being taken that the shape always approach that of a circle, an oval, or at least a diamond. Most animals can be drawn fitting into a circular border, as you can ascertain for yourself by putting a cat or a hare, etc., into a hoop.   Indent with stamped work or carve in ribbon-work, low relief, finish and polish with care, dye black, and then oil or varnish.   These are useful for

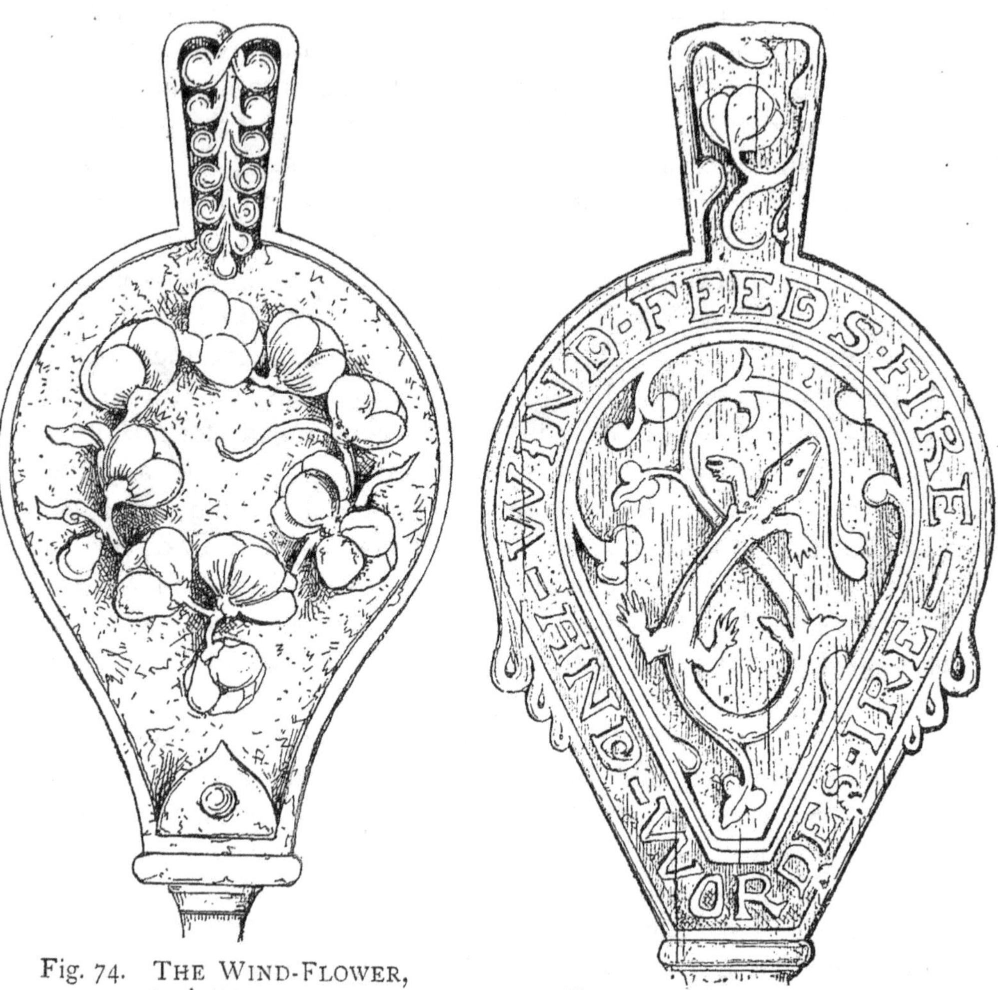

Fig. 74.   THE WIND-FLOWER,
       OR ANEMONE.

Fig. 75.   A SALAMANDER.

interposing between cups, vases, etc., and the table-cloth.   Very pretty effects may be produced by inlaying small discs of pearl or ivory to form the eyes, etc.

Lunettes and Spaces. It will often happen that there is over a chimney-piece or door, or under or over a window, a space like a semi-circle, or half an ellipse or oval, or square or rectangle of any kind, which might very well be filled in, and it will be found that, in most cases, there is nothing more appropriate than wood-carving. It will be an easy matter for anyone in the least familiar with drawing to adapt the designs in this work, or in the " Manual of Design," to such spaces.

False Sofa-backs. When a plain flat lounge or sofa is placed against a wall its appearance may be greatly improved in one of two ways. Firstly, a carpet or cloth may be hung on the wall, just matching it in size and meeting it. Secondly, and this is very effective, get boards or panels made into a piece, just as broad as the sofa is long, and from two feet to any height you please. It may reach down to the ground, or begin with the sofa. Carve it. This will seem to be the back of the sofa, or a guard for the wall; in any case it will appear very well. It may be made of separate panels, say six or eight inches by twelve or sixteen, made up into a frame. Such pieces may be placed to back any kind of furniture which rests permanently against the wall.

Door Pieces. Panels just as long as the door is wide, and from one to two, three, or even four feet across, when carved, form handsome decorations to place *above* a door; they may also be used to place above windows. Inscriptions, or simple figures with ornament, look very well on them.

Outside or Façade Pieces. Many a house, be it mansion or cottage, which seems utterly prosaic and plain, might be greatly improved if between its windows, on the outside, there could be set ornamental panels. These may be painted, carved in stone, moulded of Portland cement or other artificial stone, and in many cases carved of wood. Ornamented inscriptions in old English, and simple figures, are suitable for these panels ; in any case let those who adopt them try not to have the commonplace cupids and ornaments generally seen in mural decoration. It may not be in good form to be grotesque, but those who entirely avoid it are almost always commonplace. Fig. 76.

· *Wood or Coal Boxes.* These are square boxes with lids, to be placed by the fireplace. The coal-scuttle, with the coals, may be placed in them. In carving everything of the kind it is a good idea to introduce ornamental lettering and appropriate mottoes.

Bread Platters. These may be seen in every fancy or furnish-ing shop where wooden wares are sold. They can be much improved by carving to serve as round panels.

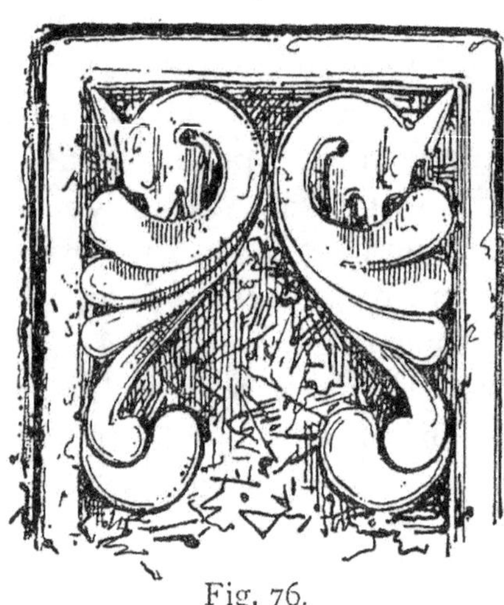

Fig. 76.

Chimney-pieces. These generally consist of pilaster panels and strips, and anybody who can execute these in detail can have them made up. It is desirable for the pupil to copy a few or many chimney-pieces, great or small, from real ones, and adopt the ornaments from them. And as they are articles which receive a great deal of wear and tear and rubbing, it may be well to re-member that too delicate finish is misplaced where scrubbing with soap and sand is sure to set in some day, and where, at any rate, dusting and other processes are inevitable. After a few years the foliage or flowers undercut to the last degree, begin to shed their leaves, and appear broken or ragged. Good flat-carving, which endures anything, is better than this, and the roses, even if in high relief, would look none the worse for being solidly though conventionally cut. A good chimney-piece and a handsome high-backed armchair can be very well executed by anybody who can do ordinary panel carving.

There is no fireplace in even the humblest cottage for which a chimney-piece may not be made. Its upper portion can in most cases be made to support shelves or a cabinet ; when in a corner these of course are triangular. Gothic or ornamented lettering may be used in the ornament. For this, proverbs or quotations relative to the fireplace are appropriate.

Beams. When the beams which support the floor above are left exposed, the room is improved by being made higher. If these beams are carved, even if it be done rudely, the whole room seems to be adorned. This is strikingly the case when the beams are stained a dark brown, and then touched up a little on the prominent points with gilding. If it be too difficult to carve the beams *in situ* or in place, it is easy to ornament them with applied carved ornaments. Pains should be taken to make these appear to be uniform with the wood.

Racks. These may be for umbrellas, hats, garments, pipes weapons, and other purposes. Great ingenuity and taste can be developed in designing them. Of one thing let the designer be very careful. Let him see that the pegs or hooks are strongly fixed and are not ornamented. I have seen such pieces of furniture, in which a four-cornered sharp-edged flower is placed once and even twice on a hook, while on others there is at the end a projection more than an inch in diameter, which is flat on the back or under side, with a sharp edge. The result is, that when a coat is hung by the loop on such a peg and is then turned or twisted once or twice, as often happens, it is almost impossible at times to get it off.

The Boss or round central projection formed a very important part or speciality in mediæval wood-carving. It can be advantageously used as a centre, and sets off to good effect surrounding flat or plain carving. It is sometimes used as a handle for chests. It is, when a simple half-circle, very easily sketched into shape. It may be formed into the head of an animal, a flower, a single curling leaf, or several leaves. The student is specially urged to copy as many as he can from Gothic designs. A boss at the bottom of a bowl, or in a saucer or *plaque*, produces a good effect, the concave surface round it making a beautiful effect of shade, which might be more fre: quently employed by picture-frame makers. This ornament, which is very easily made and very striking, is thus prepared. Get a bowl or a shallow round platter ; any turner will make one for you. Then carve from a hemisphere of wood a head or a boss of leaves or flowers, or a dragon. Round the bottom with a file to fit, and with glue and a screw fasten it to the bowl. The interior of the bowl may be polished, varnished, gilded, or ivoried.

Clock Cases. A common clock is not very expensive, and when it is properly repainted and set in a well-carved frame its value will be very much enhanced. A tower is a very good subject for a clock case.

Vestibule. The small ante-hall, between the first and second door, common in very many houses. This can be ornamented with a wainscot or dados in long panels. It is very often thus decorated in America. For cottages and country houses, or even for town mansions, such panels may be beautifully and fitly decorated with gouge-work in grooves, a flat pattern in simple cutting-in, such as any person may learn how to execute in a few hours. Fill in the pattern or cuts with dark paint, and if exposed to changes of temperament or rubbing, let it be oiled or varnished. The same work is of course as appropriate to halls as any other rooms, but the vestibule, being small, may serve for a beginning.

Staircase Balusters. These afforded inexhaustible work for the artists of the olden time, and they should be tempting to every wood-carver. It is not at all necessary that they should be strictly of open work, in lattices or rails, as beautiful objects of the kind were once often made in panels. But the carver should especially be aware of projecting leaves or crochets, as they are very apt to "catch" garments.

Garden-work. Much bold wood-carving may be executed for gardens in a great variety of forms. Stands or tables for potted flowers and tubs may be decorated, panels placed in walls, and summer-houses made in far greater variety than they are at present. Poetry supplies an infinite variety of inscriptions appropriate to gardens, which may be carved and ornamented. It is worth noting that statues of Flora and Pomona and Vertemnus in simple archaic forms were used to protect gardens and orchards among the Romans, and it would be an easy matter to carve these in low relief in panels.

Gates. The gates of country places, gardens, etc., afford a wide scope for the skill of the carver, and as they are the first objects generally seen about a house they may be most appropriately ornamented. In this, as in much other work, the art of the carpenter is combined with that of the carver. It should be, however, remembered, as regards gates, as of all decoration whatever, that anything which can ever be in any manner in the way is not beautiful, sensible, or proper. There should never be a jagged or pointed ornament wherever it can "catch" clothing.

Bedsteads. The bedstead was of old considered so appropriate for carving, that I find in an excellent old Italian work on furniture more illustrations of this article than any other. Even very simple and cheap ones may be redoubled in value by a little judicious carving.

Trays. These may be made in great variety, to contain many kinds of objects. As a rule the tray is a long shallow box, but it may be carved from one piece of wood, and is then used to carry objects in, the single piece being necessary to give it strength. If ornamented with carving the tray forms an attractive object when hung up on the wall. And it may be here remarked that one great object of all carving is, that most objects which are useful in some way shall be ornamental when not in use. We do not wish to have trays and coal-boxes in the way if they are plain, but when decorated they serve as well as pictures to ornament a room.

Coal or Wood Boxes. See Wood or Coal Boxes.

Salt Boxes, Collection Boxes. These very useful articles need not be limited as regards contents, nor confined to the kitchen or to "collection." If the part of the box which goes against the wall, or its back, be lengthened, the salt box becomes a kind of bracket. *Vide Hanging Boxes.*

Shelf-boards. It very often happens that a literary man, or draughtsman, or architect, though his work-table may be large, finds it crowded with books, etc. To find place for these the shelf-board is very convenient. It is simply a board, let us say one foot wide, placed on two supports, which lift it twelve or fifteen inches from the table. To economize room these supports may each be a square open box, in which books may be placed. The advantage of this shelf is that it may be displaced at any time when the table is cleared. A plain board in a room is not an attractive object, its edge, or even one side of it, may therefore be carved.

Brackets and Bracket Shelves. These useful objects may be made in a great variety of forms. The simplest is merely three pieces of board fastened together in a triangle. In the illustration, Fig. 77, there are five pieces. The centre of *b* slopes at an angle of 45°. Bracket shelves are made by hanging two brackets and laying a board across them. A bracket may be made on a longer board, and have two or more shelves, it then becomes a hanging rack or cabinet. Or the support may be a long strip in which pegs of wood or metal are placed, on which objects are hung. A very great variety of carved or stamped ornament may be adapted to brackets.

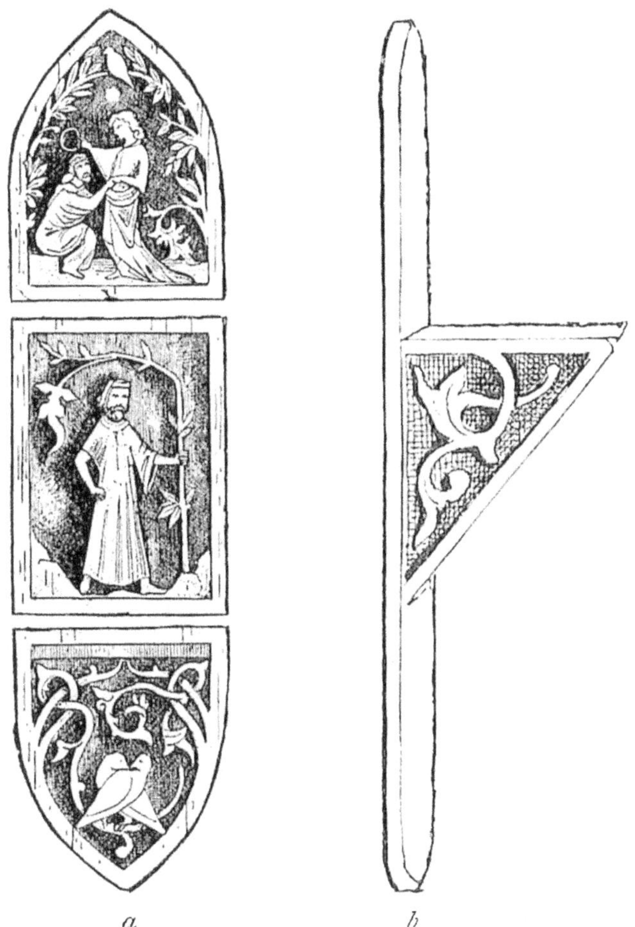

a   *b*

Fig. 77. Bracket. The Tannhäuser.

Violin and Guitar Cases. In the old times these were often elaborately carved, and thus formed an ornament, instead of being, like all now used, anything but attractive.

Handles for Drawers. The hanging or hinge style of old-

fashioned handles, now so prevalent, has the drawbacks of not
being always easy to open or " find," and of frequently breaking.
The knob, which was screwed on, was always wearing out and
getting out of order.   The best and most practical kind is made
with a square shank which passes through a square hole in the
drawer.   It has also in itself a square hole into which a square
pin is driven, which holds it fast.   Carving in very low relief may
be applied to ornament these handles, but it should never be such
as to produce positive inequalities, such as press into, or may
hurt the hand.   If the pin be slightly wedge-shaped, it can
never wear out, nor can the handle become loose, since when it
does, all that is required is to drive it in further.   A very plain
chest of drawers may be made much more attractive with a
handsome set of handles.   Handles are another form of bosses.

Applied Ornaments.   Old Roman bronze coins, such as may
be bought for two or three pence, are often quite handsome
enough to be applied with beautiful effect in caskets, tankards,
or boxes.   Lay the coin on the wood, draw its exact circle
with a pin, and do this until the line is rather deeply scratched.
Cut out the disc with great care, so that the coin may fit tightly
into it.   For this purpose very thick coins are preferable.   Let
it project a little from the surface.   Fasten it in with diamond
or Turkey cement.   Of course, medals or coins of any kind
may be used.   Make a border in the wood round the coin, and
if you like, apply other ornament to this border.   Large nails
with circular boss heads are very effective in furniture.   Chests
may be beautifully ornamented with them.

Waste-Paper Box.   A carved box is much more " sightly " and
solid than an ordinary waste-paper basket.   The box may be
carved in a basket pattern, and made rather wider at the top
than the bottom.

Borders.   Any ornament continued in a line or strip forms a
border.   A wave line, or one made of hemi-circles, joined or not

with ornaments in every compartment, is a good plan for a border. So is a vine of any kind. When the hemi-circles are squared and joined, it becomes the basis for the Greek Meander or Wall of Troy. Angles and other forms are also used. Any diaper may be repeated so as to form a border. Borders around panels and other margins, and all along the edges of boards for shelves, brackets and most of the works mentioned in this list, may be executed in highly decorative effect, and with an ease and precision diffi- cult to attain by carving, with the hammer and stamps mentioned in the first lesson. Lines are first drawn on the work as guides to place the punches to insure regularity.

Pilaster. Though this term is generally applied to what may be called a flat-sided pillar against a wall, or a flat half pillar, in wood-carving it means quite as often a per- pendicular border in relief. Like borders, pilasters are

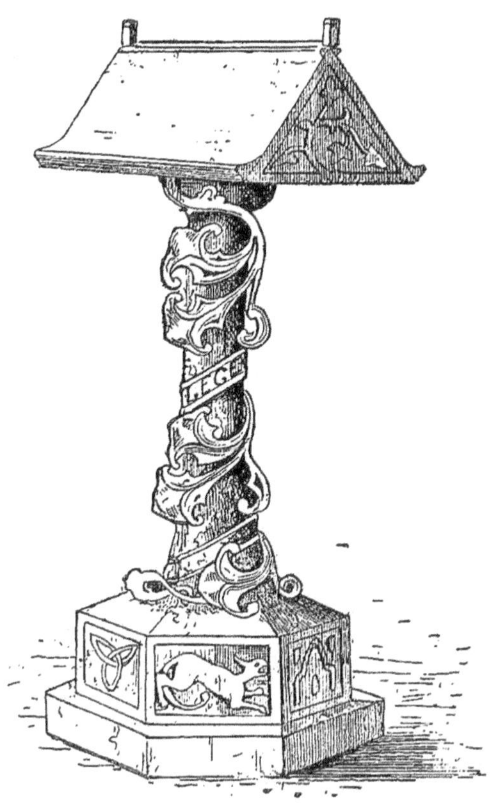

Fig. 78. LECTERN.

used in many ways in decoration, as on walls, bureaux, cabinets, sideboards, tables, or wherever a long " strip " is to be filled.

Base Moulding. This is generally a border which is the lower portion of a piece of furniture, etc. Thus, if there is a panel and frame, and under this, just over the " feet," a carved strip, it is a base moulding. Narrow fillets on these may be also decorated by stamping.

Sideboard or Buffet. A piece of furniture eminently adapted to ornament. It may be made with a back or with shelves, niches, or a cabinet placed on it instead of a back.

Alms Boxes, Money Boxes. These are made up for churches, generally after Gothic designs, and afford a wide range of design.

Lectern. A church reading desk. This has always been a favourite subject with wood-carvers, Fig. 78.

Ends of Pews. A favourite subject for carvers in the days of old, *vide* Fig. 80.

Porte-papier. A very useful article to carry paper, or a sketch-book, or to press leaves and flowers and convey them home. Take two pieces of board, from one-third to one-half an inch in thickness, and six inches by eight in size, more or less as may be desired. The paper is placed between these boards and the whole secured with a hand-strap. It is usual to carve a flower pattern on these.

Ring or Circular Boxes. Take a board, of any thickness, *e.g.* one of two inches, and make of it a disc or circle, using the steel fret saw, Fig. 16; then marking out another circle within this, saw out a ring about three-quarters of an inch in thickness. Adapt to this a bottom and lid, both, of course, also circular. It will be like what is known as a cheese box. To double the depth saw out two rings and glue them together. This will give four inches depth. Boxes may thus be made of any shape, such as a fish, and then carved.

Photograph or Mirror Frames, or Mounts. Take a piece of thin board, six inches by four or five, or any size required. Cut out of one corner of this as much as will be required for the photograph or mirror, leaving enough wood for a pattern. These have become very popular of late, Fig. 79.

Fig. 79. FRAME FOR A PHOTOGRAPH, LOOKING GLASS, ETC.

Triptych. Two folding covers or boards on hinges, intended to cover a picture or carved or enamelled or inlaid work. These triptychs may be used reversed as writing desks, or else carved on both sides, and then when open hung on the wall as ornaments. When there are only two boards, as in an album, it is called a diptych.

Encoignures. Tables made with an angle to fit into a corner of a room.

Shields. Carved in wood, these form beautiful ornaments.

Incitega. A kind of stand or table for flowers. It was generally made of rods or strips, but it may be very easily formed like a box, that is, a truncated pyramid reversed. The sides are carved.

Monopodium or Centre-table. A small circular table supported on a central stem or foot, used by the ancients at social entertainments.

Orb. A globe covered with ornaments carved in low relief. They form very effective decorations.

Finial. A terminating ornament, corresponding to a flower as a crochet does to a side leaf, Fig. 80, etc.

Coin-brackets. Brackets made to fit into the corner of a room.

Corner-cabinets. Cabinets adapted to a corner of a room. There are also coin or corner objects of furniture of all kinds.

Mouldings. These are narrow borders or strips, and are very effective in giving relief in long spaces. A good effect for a full border, a diaper ground or a broad pattern, may often be made by doubling, trebling, etc., mouldings. By using the folding mirror a segment of any moulding or border may be converted into an ornament to fill up any given space, of any shape. There are several tools specially made for cutting figures in mouldings.

Poppy-heads. There are many cases where carving may be applied with good effect to relieve bareness. " Such ornaments, generally small groups of foliage " (though often figures with leaves), " were formerly placed on the summits of bench-ends desks, and other clerical wood-work" (F. W. Fairholt, Poppy-heads can be placed, however, or adapted, to all kinds of furniture, with a variation in form, Fig. 80.

Sconce. A wall candlestick, which usually takes the form of a projecting bracketed support in wood or metal. They originated in the fifteenth century, and were generally of enriched design. They may be sawed out of boards, or carved in many forms.

Trellis-screens. These are thin boards of open lattice-work, generally made by fret-sawing and subsequent carving. They are useful to place behind windows, and for many purposes.

Tympanum. A triangular space, which may be filled in with carved ornament.

Verge or Barge-board. The gable ornament of wood-work, used extensively for houses in the fifteenth century. It affords a wide field for decoration.

Wreaths. Carved circles or rings of wood, which form beautiful ornaments, especially when hung up at intervals. They may be used for picture-frames, Fig. 81.

Acerra. A square box, on legs or supports.

Heads and Legs. When a cylinder, or square stick, or horn, or oval box, is made to rudely resemble a figure by adding to it a head and legs, this is so called.

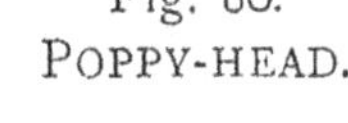

Fig. 80.
POPPY-HEAD.

Ædicula. A small house or tower, generally used as a box. Very effective and beautiful articles are thus made.

Ante-fix. Ornament carved in stone or wood, or made from terra-cotta, "to give an ornamental finish or to conceal unsightly junctions in masonry" (Fairholt). There are few country houses or cottages where they cannot be applied.

Ciborium, Synedoche. Very richly adorned receptacles in which the Host is kept. They may be imitated for cabinets. In Spanish churches they are called *custodia*.

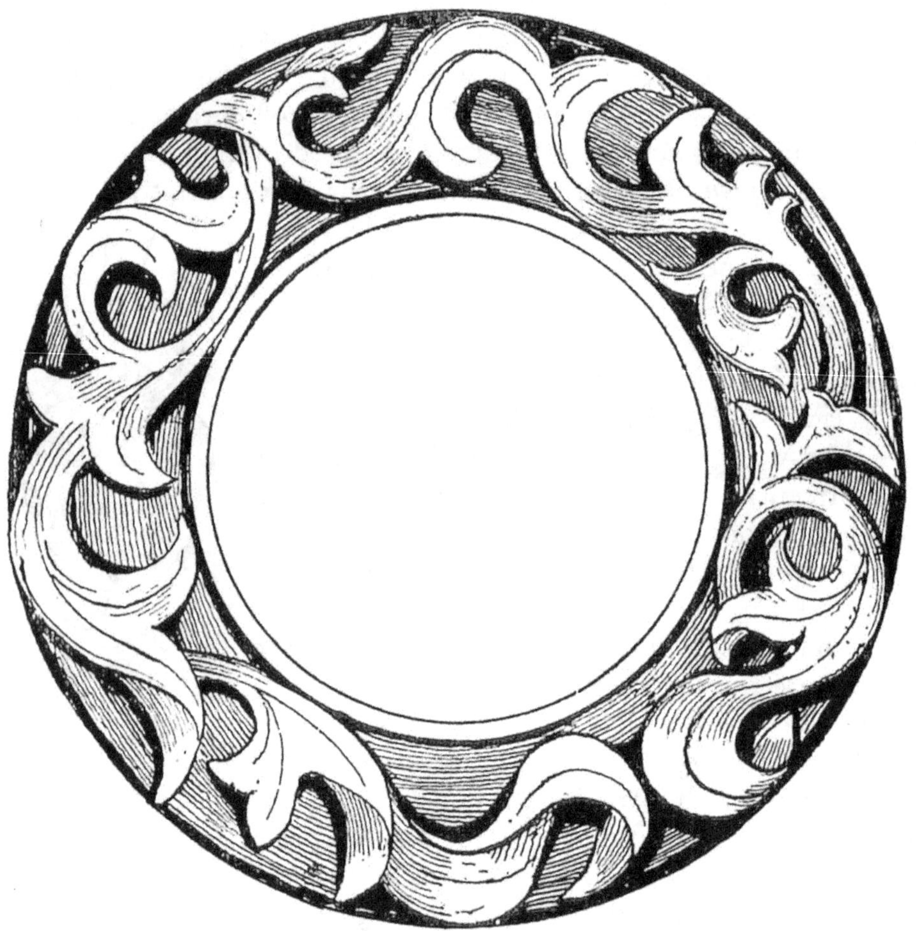

Fig. 81.   Ring-box, Wreath, or Bread Platter.

Cyma. A moulding consisting of a round and hollow conjoined, termed *cyma recta* when hollow above, and *cyma reversa* when the cavity is below.

Modillons.   Brackets in Gothic architecture, the lower portion often in the form of a grotesque animal or human being.

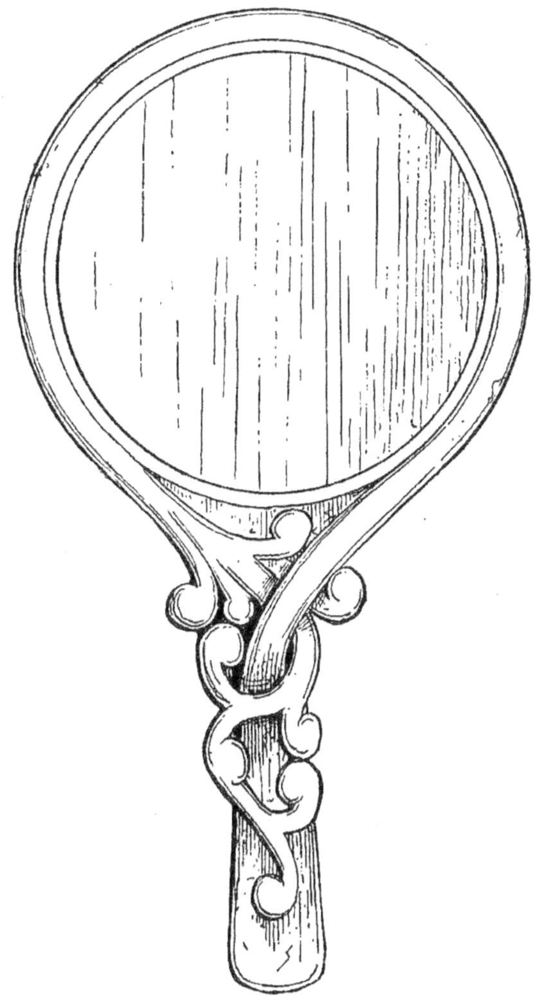

Fig. 82.   HAND MIRROR.

Hand Mirrors.   These afford an endless field for design. Fig. 82.

Echinus. The egg and tongue or egg and anchor moulding, much like the heart and dart ornament. It is easily made and is very effective. Faces may be cut on the " eggs."

Outlines. Figures of men, animals, etc., cut or sawed out of boards, and either painted or carved. They are common in Italian churches. They form very effective hanging ornaments. Birds can be adapted to beautiful outlines.

Hammer Beam. The projecting end of a beam, often carved.

Hood Moulding. The moulding which covers or surmounts a door or window on the outside, forming a sort of hood or weather-guard. It is also called a dripstone or weather mould-ing. It can be beautifully ornamented, and thus becomes a striking decoration.

Impost. The horizontal moulding on the summit of a pillar from which the arch springs.

Console. (French.) Brackets in furniture.

Perfume Chests. Boxes with perforated lids in which is kept *pot-pourri* of rose leaves, or a mixture of powdered orris-root and spice.

Churns. A carved churn is a fanciful ornament, used to contain papers, etc. The handle is fixed to the cover and serves to lift it.

Handles for Bowls, Cups, or Boxes. These are sawn from board from one half to an inch in thickness, and then fastened to the bowl or box, generally with screws. When gracefully or quaintly shaped they convert any ordinary bowl or tankard, with very little trouble, to an attractive ornament. They are almost peculiar to Sweden and Norway, where they may be seen in museums in very great variety.

Bark Frames. A curious and striking ornament may be made in this manner. Take a piece of cork, oak, or other bark, which may be a foot in length by six inches. Make in it an oval or circle, in which carve any subject. The writer once had an image of the Virgin thus carved, which was much admired. Dark brown bark is much improved by having gilding roughly spread on its projecting points. If the ground of the carving be gilt and the bark left in its natural condition the effect will also be good.

Three-legged, or *Milking Stools*. These are commonly carved on the seat. Ornaments may be carved and better applied as in Fig. 83.

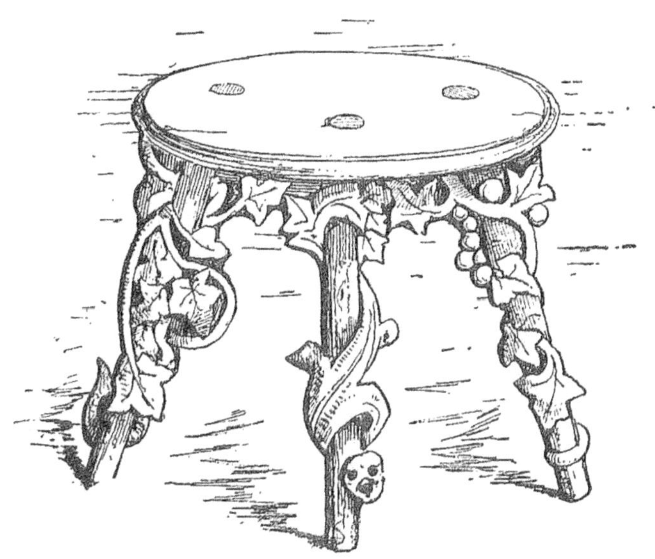

Fig. 83. THREE-LEGGED STOOL.

INDEX.